HOW TO PLAY
SNOOKER

REX WILLIAMS

TREASURE PRESS

Contents

First published in Great Britain in 1982 by
The Hamlyn Publishing Group Limited

This edition published in 1988 by
Treasure Press
59 Grosvenor Street
London W1

ISBN 1 85051 303 1

Printed by Mandarin Offset in Hong Kong

Acknowledgements

The diagrams in this book are by Peter F.
Chaplin. The photographs of the author in
Chapters 1–3 are by M. Athar Chaudhry. Other
photographs including Alex Higgins (pages 4/5)
and Terry Griffiths (pages 62/63) are by Sporting
Pictures (UK) Ltd, London.

This book is a slightly amended version of
'Snooker: How to become a Champion',
by William Luscombe Publisher Limited in 1975

Chapter One
The Basics

Most players who have played competitively, even at the lowest level, have harboured ambitions or just daydreams to become a champion, perhaps not World Professional champion but possibly champion of their local league or winner of their club handicap. Comparatively few have ever done anything positive about it, simply playing on year after year, ingraining bad habits more deeply, making the same mistakes. The fact that you are reading this book at all implies that you are different, that you are actually doing something more practical than just hoping for a miracle.

But to what extent are you prepared to put yourself out? Are you going to skim through this, picking up a tactical hint here and there, filing the information away in your mind for the time that the relevant situation crops up in a match? That is better than nothing but it will not achieve much in comparison with the man who actually gets on a table to practise the positions I discuss. Throughout my career, I have spent many hours in solo practice because if you do this systematically you will improve at a much greater rate than if you simply play one of your friends for two hours every night.

Of course, even this latter method should produce *some* improvement simply through the number of balls you hit but without some more systematic practice most players reach a certain level and stick there, though even these players, as I hope to show, could sometimes achieve better results through clearer thinking or better choice of shot without any dramatic improvement in technique.

Billiards and snooker are probably the most technical and in many ways the most difficult games in the world although there is less coaching for them than for any other sport.

My main emphasis will be on snooker because this is now much the more popular game, but there are many areas where what I write will be equally relevant to both games. This is particularly true of this opening chapter on the basics of grip, cueing and stance. Get these right and you will have taken a big step towards becoming a good player: get them wrong and you will be limiting your potential right from the start. For this kind of instruction, words mean relatively little without photographs, so study the photographs in this section very carefully.

First, the grip (see Figure 1), one of the simpler things to acquire, I believe. All that is required, in fact, is for you to pick up the cue as if you were going to hit someone over the head with it.

Second, the bridge (see Figure 2): push your left arm out straight and place your left-hand on the table. Cock the thumb to form a bridge between thumb and first finger and grip the cloth firmly with all four fingers. Standing sideways to the table, place the cue in your bridge and, in a manner of speaking, you are ready to play. Of course, there is a little more to it than that. For one thing your success depends a great deal on delivering the cue through straight. How do you acquire this proficiency in cueing? How can cueing be grooved?

If you want a short answer — practice. But if you are doing certain basic things wrongly, all the practice in the world will not make much difference.

First of all, make sure that your stance is all it should be (see Figures 3–6). Your rear leg ought to be straight but your weight should be forward and your front leg bent.

Some players play with both legs bent but I do not recommend this. The reason for this may be easily seen if you conduct a simple test. When you have adopted your stance ask a friend to give you a slight sideways push. If you have a firm rock-like stance, you will hardly

Fig. 1 **The Grip:** Having picked up the cue as if to hit someone over the head, I bring it to as horizontal a position as possible to strike the ball. I do not grip the cue at the very end but leave a few inches showing. The arm from wrist to elbow is vertical — emphasised by the angle of the cuff link on my shirt.

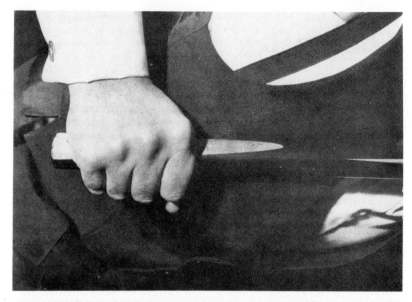

Fig. 2 **The Bridge:** The thumb is cocked, the four other fingers gripping the cloth firmly. The cue travels through a channel made between the thumb and first finger. The fingers being widely spread, the cue actually travels across the first finger just above the middle knuckle. The palm cannot be flat because the knuckles could not be raised high enough to make the bridge, but the weight is evenly distributed for maximum stability as the shot is made.

Fig. 3 (opposite) **The Stance—Frontal:** The frontal view of my stance emphasizes the straight line which is made by my cue, left eye and the point of my right elbow. Out of view another straight line is formed on the vertical by my right arm from wrist to elbow. This straight line is desirable because it is the best way of co-ordinating the aim (through the eyes) with the part of my body which has to execute the aiming i.e. the arm) and the implement used by the arm (i.e. the cue)

Most players make this alignment between the cue and the point of the elbow by sighting equally with both eyes so that the cue runs

move at all. But if you have a 'two legs bent' or other unsteady stance you will very nearly fall over.

You will need a mirror to ascertain whether your stance is perfect in one way, namely this: shoulder, elbow and hand should form a straight line and should be in line with the cue. However, don't worry too much about this point as very few of even the very best amateurs have cue actions which measure up to the ideal. Unless you have almost unlimited time and patience it is unlikely to pay you to spend too much time acquiring this line.

Figures 7–9 all have a bearing on good cueing though the vital elements of relaxation and rhythm are difficult to convey in still photographs. Don't grip the cue as if your life depended on it. If you grip the cue too tightly the muscles become tense and stiff so that the cue arm cannot move with 100 per cent freedom. I recommend a short practice period of about twenty minutes before important matches to work some of the tension out of the system.

But don't hold the cue too floppily either, for consistent potting requires a firm but not too rigid hold.

Here is a tip about firmness of cue-hold. Put your cue down flat on the table bed. The correct amount of strength with which to hold your cue is that which is just sufficient to pick the cue up. It is, for instance, impossible to pick your cue up with merely two fingers and, therefore, the 'finger tips' cue hold is not to be recommended.

The line from wrist to elbow should be perpendicular with a slight tendency forward, that is, the angle between the upper and lower arm should be slightly less than ninety degrees.

Rhythm is vital, not only to a break, but to an individual shot. To obtain a rhythmic action, it is necessary to form a habit of addressing the cue-ball a few times preparatory to striking it. This preliminary process is known as 'feathering'. Some players 'feather' almost imperceptibly, drawing back their cue only a centimetre or two (about half an inch) before drawing it back 15 centimetres (six inches) or so for the final blow. In my opinion, the preliminary feathering at the ball should involve more decisive movements.

If the feathering involves a backward and forward movement of only a centimetre or so (half an inch), it leads to a certain stodginess in the cue-action. However, a more decisive feathering, of up to say eight centimetres (three inches), leads to a more fluent action. In fact, in my younger days, I used a metronome in my practice for this purpose. Be careful, on the other hand, not to make the along the chin directly between the eyes. But sighting is a natural thing and I have always sighted with my cue underneath my left eye because this is 'my master eye' and the right follows it. I am in good company here because Joe Davis used to do the same.

In a sense, players whose left eye is stronger than their right tend to be more compact but if your eyes are of equal strength it would be a mistake to try to sight with your left eye because this would be completely unnatural.

Fig. 4 **The Stance – Rear View:** The angle of this picture again illustrates the line-up between cue, elbow and left eye. Note that I am gripping the cue firmly but not rigidly.

Fig. 5 **The Stance – Side View (1):** Note how the line between wrist and right elbow is perpendicular. The cue is travelling as near the horizontal as possible and I am as low on the cue as it is possible to be.

Fig. 6 **Side View (2):** This illustrates many of the points I have brought out in the previous photographs but emphasises most of all the position of the legs and feet. The left leg is bent with my left foot pointing directly along the line of the shot. The right leg is straight and braced with the right foot comfortably positioned to give me balance. My weight is on the front leg (the left) leaning forward into the shot.

feathering movements too long – you will make slower-than-medium-paced shots more difficult; faster-than-medium no easier.

Let us assume, then, that you are feathering at the cue-ball preparatory to hitting it. When you have drawn the cue back for the last time there should be a very slight hesitation, not enough to disrupt your rhythm but sufficient for your eyes to switch from the cue-ball back to the object-ball for the last time, to make any fractional adjustment that may be necessary in your cueing – and by fractional I mean the very slightest adjustment, hundredths of a centimetre or an inch. However, if your cue action is a good one and you have kept perfectly still on the stroke you will very often find that you are hitting the object-ball exactly where you want to. If this is so, you have only to thrust your cue through good and straight to ensure the success of your shot, assuming you have assessed the angle correctly.

There is one last point to remember and it is a very important one: stillness on the shot. The only part of the body that ought to move when you are playing a shot is your cue

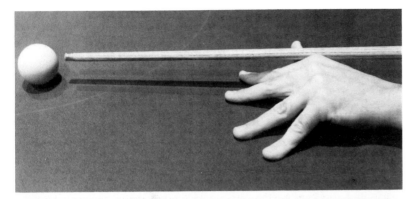

Fig. 7 **Cueing (1):** Placing the bridge hand some 15 centimetres (six inches) from the ball, the cue makes a number of preliminary addresses at the cue-ball, building up rhythm prior to the actual shot. With each preliminary address the cue-tip approaches within a couple of centimetres or so (about half an inch) of the ball.

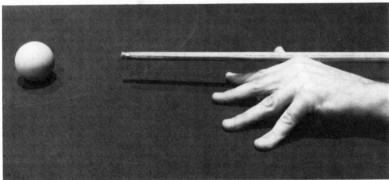

Fig. 8 **Cueing (2):** When you have completed your preliminary addresses, draw the cue back and hesitate fractionally before thrusting it through. This picture shows the cue at the full extent of my backswing. My backswing is shorter than some players who withdraw their cue almost level with the tips of their fingers. The shorter the backswing you can achieve while still being able to generate plenty of power, the better equipped you will be, since the longer a backswing is, the more chance there is of something going wrong.

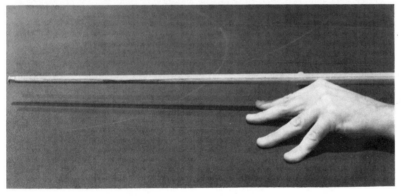

Fig. 9 **Cueing (3):** As the stroke is made, it is most important that the cue should hit straight through the ball. As this picture shows, my own cue has preserved the same horizontal line it had both in my preliminary addresses and my backswing. Note also the length of the follow-through.

arm. Above all, keep your head down. The harder you hit the ball the more difficult it is to keep your head down. So, every time you have to hit a ball hard just pay a little more attention to this particular point.

What about shots to practise? The obvious shot is the over-the-spot one illustrated in Figure 10, Shot 1. However, I think that extended practice at this shot is useful to beginners. I still use it myself but only as a brief 'check-up' shot. It is a good idea to do it for two or three minutes, hitting the cue-ball at varying speeds but a better practice shot for players al-

ready beyond the novice stage is Shot 2 shown in the diagram.

Place any ball on the blue spot and put the cue-ball on the baulk line so that you have a dead straight pot. Keep practising this pot until you can get it consistently then line up a series of straight pots into the other top corner pocket (as shown in Figure 10, Shot 3). If you can keep stunning balls in from this position there is nothing much wrong with your cue action.

For players with some experience – that is most of those who read this book – these early chapters offer not so much instructions from scratch as

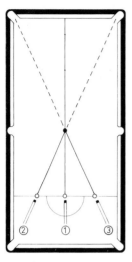

Fig. 10

an opportunity to put some element in your game right. Even if you feel reasonably happy with your stance and cue action re-read the previous paragraphs to see if there isn't some small point you can pick up.

Do you find, for instance, that you unintentionally, but consistently, strike the cue-ball slightly to the left or right of centre? If you are consistently striking to the right, your right foot may have come round too far so that you are standing more square to the table than you should. If you are consistently striking to the left, it could be too much to the back. However good you are, a few minutes stroking over the spots or some long straight pots are the best check-up. It is worth experimenting to get these matters right because if you cannot strike the cue-ball accurately there are serious limits to the accuracy you can expect in striking the object-ball.

Striking the object-ball is of course what the games are all about and the first thing any budding snooker player wants to know is how to pot. Some enthusiasts have produced the most intriguing theories about potting but I will say straightaway how essential it is to try and play snooker the simple and instinctive way. The surest way to put yourself off is to become obsessed with technique and theory.

There are, however, certain basic points of technique which have to be mastered and ingrained in the player so deeply that he observes them without ever having to think.

The 'sighting' of a ball begins just as you stop walking round the table. You stand for a second behind the line of the shot, assess the angle and take your stance. You should be able to assess the angle of the shot with enough precision for you to place your feet in the right place. Certain minor adjustments of aim may be necessary but these should not be enough to involve changing the position of the feet or leaning even fractionally off balance. If either of these become necessary through initial misjudgement of the angle, get up and start again.

As my chin goes down to my cue to sight the shot, my eyes look first at the cue-ball and then constantly switch back and forth from the cue-ball, looking at the cue-ball on the backswing, the object-ball on the forward swing. At the beginning of the final backswing I hesitate momentarily, just long enough to switch my eyes from cue-ball to object-ball and then, with my eyes on the object-ball, swing the cue smoothly through.

This momentary hesitation – hardly longer than it takes to blink an eye – is, I am convinced, one of the real 'secrets' of the game, for bringing the cue back and then forward in one continuous movement often leads to a jerk in the cue-action.

All my sighting is done instinctively. I never think of a shot as five-sevenths ball or, except in general terms, half-ball.

It is only through practice and trial and error that you will learn where to hit a ball to pot it. If you have particular difficulty with one kind of pot set the same pot up a couple of dozen times. If you keep missing the pot by about the same margin each time either your cueing has gone wrong or you have assessed the angle wrongly. If it is your assessment that is at fault and the object-ball is hitting the cushion eight centimetres (three inches) to the left of the pocket each time, try to imagine the pocket is eight centimetres (three inches) further to the right. If you then start to pot the ball you have taken the first step in picking out the correct angle.

During the preliminary cueing to the stroke the eyes are constantly moving from cue-ball to object-ball. On the last backswing preliminary to striking the cue-ball, the eyes should switch from cue-ball to object-ball and remain there until the completion of the stroke. The more you play, the easier you will find it to assess potting angles almost automatically. Successful potting involves a co-ordinating process between your eyes and a cue controlled by your arm. It is not a bit of use picking out the right potting angles if your cue action is unreliable.

Chapter Two
Other Bridges

Even novices do not have to play long before they realize that they cannot use the orthodox bridge all the time. Cushions or other balls often interfere with the placing of the standard bridge so it is a good idea to become accustomed as soon as possible to the other bridges you will need to employ.

In particular, study the photographs in this and the next chapter and the captions to them (Figures 12–21, 27–29, 32, 33) – and practise with them until each bridge feels natural and familiar. Many league-standard players do not give themselves the best possible chance with certain shots simply because they do not bridge correctly in certain positions. Many more contort themselves into all sorts of shapes or even overreach to a degree where they have no control over the cue at all, in preference to using the rest. Get rid of these bad habits right at the start. The longer you let them go on the harder it is to break them.

Everybody has trouble when the cue-ball is either tight under the cushion or immediately in front of another ball. In both cases, it is possible to strike only the top part of the cue-ball and this means you have to rely entirely on accurate plain ball striking. As the cue-ball will drift from its intended line if it is carrying side, it is imperative to be able to strike the cue-ball in the middle.

Most players will be familiar with the old exercise of 'shooting over the spots' (see Figure 10) to test true cueing. Carrying this test a stage further, place the cue-ball tight on the baulk cushion, immediately behind the brown spot and play over the spots at varying speeds until you can get the cue-ball to return straight and true.

When you can do this reasonably well, place an object-ball in the middle of the baulk cushion and the cue-ball immediately in front of it and repeat the exercise. Do this for a few minutes and then move on to the shots I have shown in Figure 11.

Figure 11, Shot 1 is a straight black off its spot. This shot has to be played fairly slowly and demands perfect cueing and, I may say, a perfectly true table. As the butt of the cue must be slightly raised for this shot, you will tend to be looking into the bed of the table rather than directly at the object-ball, as you would be for a normal shot. Therefore, even more than you do normally, size up the angle of the pot before you get down on your shot.

For this shot I have drastically cut down the length of my preliminary addresses to the cue-ball so that I now have hardly any backswing at all. It is harder than usual to keep still on this shot because you are looking into the bed of the table and therefore cannot see the result of your shot without looking up. It is only natural, especially when the shot is a vital one, for you to want to see quickly whether you have got it or not, but unless your self-discipline is strong enough to keep absolutely still for a few seconds you will find yourself jerking your head up and missing the shot.

After practising potting the black with the cue-ball on the cushion, move it six or seven centimetres (two or three inches) to the left or right in turn to vary the angle. When you have done this, go back to the straight pot but put another ball tight on the side cushion and the cue-ball in front of it and start again.

However much you practise, you must not expect to get this sort of shot every time, but when you feel you have attained a reasonable level of success, move on to Figure 11, Shot 2, first playing this very awkward slow pot from the side cushion, and then more awkward still, over the ball.

Nobody can hope to play successfully over an intervening ball without a reasonably firm bridge and there are two main sources of 'wobble' one has

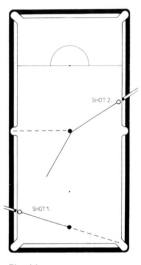

Fig. 11

Fig. 12 **Supplementary Bridges (1):** When I cannot place my bridge on the table in the normal way without feeling cramped and awkward, I favour the loop bridge illustrated here. The loop is formed by folding the first finger over the thumb to leave a hole for the cue to travel through. Note that the remaining fingers are gripping the table firmly while the rest of the hand from palm to wrist is lying flat on the top of the cushion and cushion rail.

Fig. 13 **Supplementary Bridges (2):** This picture shows the loop bridge from another angle. This shows that the loop is loose enough for the cue to travel through it, but not so loose that the cue will wobble about.

Fig. 14 **Supplementary Bridge (3):** When the cue-ball is slightly nearer the cushion than the positions shown in Figs. 12 and 13, it becomes necessary to bring the bridge hand further back. I therefore place the bridge hand on the cushion and use another variety of the loop bridge, this time forming the loop only with the first finger.

  Note that the first and second fingers are keeping the cue on line.

Fig. 15 **Supplementary Bridges (4):** This position is one in which the cushion rail prevents me from making my normal bridge. Here, I again resort to the loop bridge between thumb and first finger but on this occasion support it with only two fingers on the table and my little finger on the cushion rail.

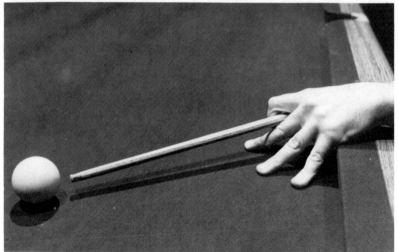

Fig. 16 **Bridging Over A Ball:** When bridging over an intervening ball, the bridge hand must of course be raised. Strive for maximum stability through four fingers gripping the table. When the cue-ball is very near the intervening ball I am able, through my countless hours of practice, to get the cue to travel extremely close to the top of the intervening ball. When the cue-ball is slightly further from the intervening ball without there being enough distance,between them to place my bridge, I would move my bridge hand slightly nearer the intervening ball.

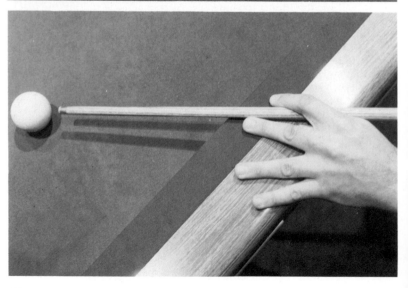

to guard against. One arises, inevitably, when the palm of the hand is taken from the table to provide the necessary elevation for striking the cue-ball without commiting a foul. In this case, wobble can be minimized by spreading the fingers widely and making a conscious attempt to grip the cloth. As one has to stand more upright because the butt of the cue has to be raised to play the shot, one's weight inevitably comes forward. The left elbow should be slightly bent.

The other source of wobble is an unduly long bridge. A very long bridge feels unnatural for ordinary strokes but it is even more awkward when the bridge cannot be supported by having the palm on the table. Therefore, make your bridge as near as possible to the intervening ball.

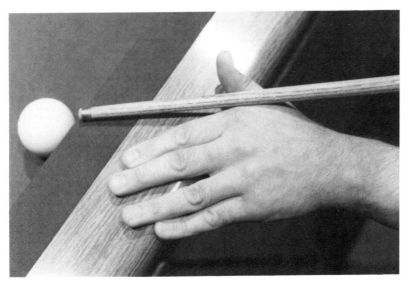

Fig. 17 **Supplementary Bridges (5)**: This picture illustrates the position even professionals dread. The cue-ball is tight under the cushion and therefore only the top part of the cue-ball can be struck by the cue. In order to bring the bridge hand a comfortable distance from the cue-ball, many players bridge simply with their finger tips on the cushion rail. This, however, causes a great deal of instability and consequent lack of accuracy in striking, so I always make sure that my fingers (up to the middle knuckles anyway) are resting on the cushion rail. Because of the restricted striking area on the cue-ball the bridge has to be raised a fraction so that the stroke is made not horizontally as usually, but slightly downward.

Fig. 18 **Awkward Positions (1):** This stance is commonly used by players of modest standard in preference to the stance illustrated in Fig. 19. The weight is taken by the left leg rather than the table, while the right leg hangs free in the air. It is very difficult indeed to remain perfectly still on the shot in this somewhat ungainly position and the only time that I would consider using it would be if there were balls between the middle and baulk pockets which prevented me putting my left leg on the table and using the stance in Fig. 19.

Fig. 19 **Awkward Positions (2):** There will be certain shots which cannot be reached with the ordinary stance but which can be reached without the use of the rest, as here. With my left leg hoisted on to the cushion rail, my weight is being taken by the table. My right foot is simply touching the floor to conform with the rules but does not have any weight upon it. Because my weight is so firmly placed there is no difficulty about keeping still as I play the shot.

Fig. 20 **Awkward Positions (3):** In this shot many players would be content simply to reach over with both feet remaining on the floor. The snag with this is that one's cueing alignment tends to alter if one plays with one's arm too far from one's body. Therefore, I lift my right leg and let the table take the weight of my body. My left leg is taking no weight but my foot of course remains in contact with the floor. Without placing my body in this way it would be impossible to preserve that vital straight line between the point of the right elbow, the right shoulder, the sighting point (in my case the left eye), the cue and the middle of the cue-ball.

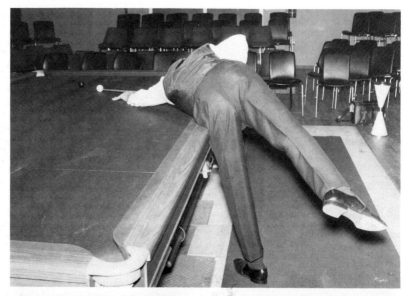

You should also try to control the cue so that it misses the intervening ball by only a fraction of an inch as it strikes at the cue-ball. A small point worth remembering about your bridge is to keep your finger nails cut short. Long nails makes it more difficult for you to grip the cloth with the flesh of your fingers.

When actually playing the shot, try to do without most preliminary addresses to the cue-ball and use little or no backswing. After I have sighted the angle at which I am trying to hit the object-ball, I keep my eyes as much as possible on the cue-ball (see Figure 16) for when the butt of the cue is raised, central striking is even more important than usual. The most important thing of all with this shot is to keep still.

Finally, if the shot is particularly important, the temptation to move is all the greater. So in such cases concentrate even more consciously on keeping perfectly still.

Chapter Three
Screw, Stun and Side

No one has a hope of progressing even to a reasonable league standard without some rudimentary command of the basic spins of the game: screw, stun and side. I have known some league players win more than they lose simply through determination, some potting ability and the ability to stop the cue-ball dead through striking it below centre, but unless your ambitions rise above this I cannot imagine why you should be reading this book!

Many average players see professionals using screw, stun and side and immediately conclude that such skills are completely outside their league. While it is true that the degree of control professionals have in these departments takes years to acquire, it is still better to have *some* command of these skills than none at all. But if you are determined to improve your game in this respect ask yourself first whether your equipment is giving you a fair chance. Many shots will be beyond your range, however good your cue action may be, if you have a poor tip.

When you have twenty apparently identical tips in front of you, how can you tell which are likely to be the best?

The first thing to do is to drop them one by one out of your fingers at a height of a few centimetres (inches) on to a wooden table. If the tip sounds very hard or very soft when dropped in this way, then I discard it. A hard tip will never become softer as you play with it; a soft tip will usually, in time, become a little harder but rarely, if ever, turn out completely satisfactory. One good test is to press your fingernail into the side of the tip. If it gives too much, it is too soft.

When I have picked out a tip, I put it in a clamp at the family printing works. This reduces the height of the tip by about 20 per cent and shortens the playing-in period. I then put the tip on either with a wafer or very strong glue. If the tip is too big, I turn the cue upside down so that I can cut downwards round the edges with a very sharp knife. I then sandpaper and file the rough edges.

Every time I put a new one on, I dread the first week or so because it seems to have so little 'feel', but as I play more I find myself gradually getting used to it and building up a nicely domed tip.

It is, of course, odds on a miscue if you try to screw back with a flat tip, so that the sooner your tip acquires a noticeable dome the better. I file my tip to get this dome but it is a good idea to get an old ball in your hand and keep tapping it round your tip for several minutes, just off centre most of the time, to bed the tip down and build up the desired dome shape. I also use my file to press it firmly into the playing surface of the tip to break up accretions of chalk so that I can reduce the risk of a miscue.

When your tip is nicely domed

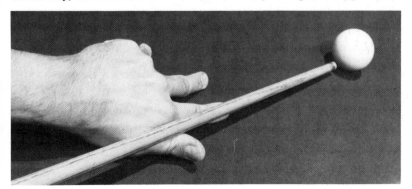

Fig. 21 **The Bridge For Screwing:** To play a screw shot, it is necessary to strike low on the cue-ball. Since it is also desirable to maintain a horizontal cue action I tilt my bridge to the right so that the thumb is resting on the bed of the table. Although the weight of the bridge thus becomes unevenly distributed, I still make sure that I grip the cloth with all my fingers to attain maximum stability.

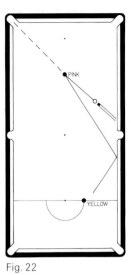

Fig. 22

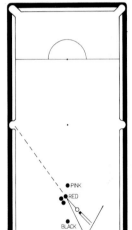

Fig. 23

Fig. 24

(and is kept chalked) it should enable you to use screw, stun and side with confidence.

However, before tackling the mechanics of the screw shot there is just one more important point to consider: the need to adjust your bridge so that the cue's horizontal relationship with the table bed can be preserved, even though the tip will be addressing a lower point on the cue-ball. Figure 21 shows me doing this.

Players who have been trying to screw back for years without much success may well find that this is simply because they are not varying their standard bridge. Instead of retaining a horizontal action they are striking downwards at the cue-ball with consequent loss of accuracy and control.

Novices who are learning to screw back should place a ball on the blue spot with the cue-ball about 30 centimetres (a foot or so) behind it so that they can play to pot the object-ball into one middle pocket while screwing the cue-ball back into the other. I will assume that you have mastered this and are ready to try something a little more ambitious.

Everybody knows that if cue-ball is struck centrally or above it will rotate forwards in the normal manner one would expect. If the cue-ball is struck low, the force of the initial blow will, of course, send the cue-ball forward but with the significant difference that it will be skidding along or rotating backwards. If the cue-ball then comes into contact with any substantial part of another ball, the backspin will make the cue-ball spring back, either straight or at an angle, instead of running through the object-ball in the normal way.

Figure 22 is what is known as a deep screw. This kind of shot is possible only if the object-ball is not too far away and if the cue-ball is struck quite hard. But I ask players to remember that there is a world of difference between a powerfully controlled swing and a tremendous sledgehammer lunge. The most important point to keep in mind is to hit clean through the cue-ball. Quite a good test of cueing on these shots is to make sure that your cue is resting on your bridge even after the most

powerful shot. All too often you find players giving a convulsive jerk as they hit the ball and finish up with their cue in the light shade and their head goodness knows where.

In Figure 22, the last red has been taken and you are on a slight angle for potting the pink. Use no side for this stroke but make sure you strike the cue-ball low enough and hard enough to finish in the good position on the yellow which is shown in the diagram.

Some players complain that they do all the right things and yet do not obtain as much screw as they would like. For them, here is another tip. Get hold of a set of billiards balls, select the spot-ball and line up one of the other balls for a suitable pot. Then manoeuvre the spot-ball until you have got the spot in exactly the place you wish your tip to hit.

Put plenty of chalk on your cue and play the shot. If you then examine the spot-ball and find that the spot is not covered with a just noticeable blob of chalk, you can be sure that you have not struck the cue-ball where you intended. If so, keep practising until you can strike correctly and consistently.

Figure 23 shows another powerful screw shot, though not quite as powerful as Figure 22. The red nearest the pink spot is pottable but a plain ball shot will involve kissing another red and consequent loss of position. However, if a screw shot is played in the manner shown on the diagram, the other red will not be touched. This shot, too, does not require any side.

Figure 24 should not be played as hard as Figures 22 and 23 but it should nevertheless be played crisply and firmly. A hopeful prod is no good at all.

In this shot, two reds are left and the man in play has a nearly straight black. The correct shot is a screw back off the black into a good position to pot red no. 1 into the same pocket. It is a good thing with this shot to have a little practice at potting the black plumb into the middle of the pocket and to be sure that you do not use the side cushion jaw.

If the black is potted off the left-hand jaw of the pocket – that is, the side cushion part of it – then, of course, the cue-ball having hit the black fuller, will come back straighter, thus ruining the chance of getting the desired perfect position on red no. 1.

At short distances the professional and top-class amateur often decide which side of the pocket to pot the ball into. From a positional point of view it can make all the difference and it is surprising what a little practice in this direction can do to bring a little extra polish to your game.

The main difference between stun and screw is that while screw is the art of bringing the cue-ball back, stun is the art of stopping it dead. Of course, when the cue-ball contacts the object-ball at an angle, stun cannot stop the ball dead. In this case, stun can be taken to mean an intermediate stage between screw and the plain ball shot.

The place that one chooses to hit on the cue-ball to apply stun varies according to the distance the cue-ball is from the object-ball. If, for example, the two balls are close together, as I have shown in Figure 25, Shot 2, it is possible to strike exactly centre and still stop the cue-ball running through.

A great many players, when playing stun shots, are under the impression that the cue-ball must be struck very deep. Except when the object-ball is 2½ metres (eight or nine feet) away this is not so.

In Figure 25, Shot 1, the cue-ball should be struck slightly below

centre, crisply and centrally, with sufficient strength to bring it back in a position to pot the next red without having to disturb the other red. If you strike lower than dead centre, the cue-ball will take a wider angle from the object-ball and go more towards the side cushion, thus reducing the margin in which you will be able to get on the pottable red without having to disturb the one next to it. Do not use side for this shot. Some people think a little left-hand side is an asset. It isn't. It is the best way to pull the cue-ball near to, or on to, a side cushion.

In Figure 26, the black is not quite straight. If you play a plain ball run through, the black comes back on its spot and prevents you from potting the last red. The correct shot here is a stun aiming to flick the red ball thinly (on the side which is nearest the black) and knock it towards the pocket.

The important point to remember is to be careful not to strike the cue-ball too low. If you do this, the cue-ball will come back fairly straight and flick the side of the red which is facing baulk. The red will be knocked on to the top cushion and the cue-ball will finish somewhere near the side cushion – a safe position. Thus, in this position, it is far better to contact the red too thin than too thick. If a thin contact is obtained the cue-ball will bounce off the top cushion and off again because the red had not been contacted thickly enough to take

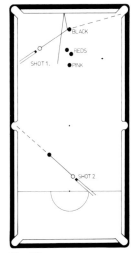

Fig. 25

Fig. 26

Fig. 27 **Using The Rest: (1)**
The Grip: When using the rest, one's stroke is made with a sideways action which of course demands a different grip on the cue. Fig. 27 shows me gripping my cue primarily with my thumb and first two fingers with the knuckles of my two other fingers giving a further measure of support. My eyes are directly behind the line of the shot but, because of the sideways action needed, my right elbow is at an angle to my cue instead of behind it. My left hand simply holds the rest firmly on the table.

Make sure that the cue follows through straight and that the sideways cue action does not bring the cue across the ball.

Fig. 28 **Using The Rest: (2) The Stroke:** Most rest heads have a 'tall way' and 'short way' up. I prefer to use the rest 'short way' up. The rest head should be placed about 20 centimetres (seven or eight inches) from the cue-ball and the cue should make a number of rhythmic preliminary addresses before the stroke itself is played.

Fig. 29 **The Spider:** a most awkward implement to use though sometimes there is no alternative. Place within three centimetres (one inch) or so of the intervening ball and get the tip of the cue to pass within a fraction of an inch of it as it strikes the cue-ball. It is an advantage for your eyes to be as much above the stroke as possible. Seldom do I try anything but a slow shot from this position, since only by restricting the movement of the cue to seven or eight centimetres (two or three inches) can one hope for a measure of accuracy or even avoid a foul shot. This is the one shot when I keep my eyes on the cue-ball when striking.

Fig. 30

ball in the centre without any side. When playing this stroke it is essential that the cue should follow well through. Hit crisply and straight and the cue-ball should run through enough to finish in a good position for the black but not enough to go anywhere near the pocket.

At the very worst, the pink is struck hard enough for it to come well away from the pocket should the pot be missed. You have a far better chance of safety this way than if you play the slow trickle. When you are actually playing the shot, however, thoughts of failure should not enter your mind. Once you have decided to play a shot you should be convinced you are going to get it. This shot is not all that easily mastered. It takes practice but not as much as you might think.

I need hardly mention, however, that you should not play this shot if you require only the pink to win. You forget entirely about playing position on the black and concentrate 100 per cent on the pot. The pot itself is surer if you strike the cue-ball lower. Do this and stun the cue-ball dead as it contacts the pink. Joe Davis once had this shot against me in a *News of the World* tournament. The pink was straight and the cue-ball was not far from it.

Even so, needing one ball to win, he took no chances but stunned the pink in and did not try for position on the black. He made 101 per cent certain of winning the game – and I would have done the same.

If you are going to use side, make up your mind to do so before you get down to play the shot. The worst

much speed off the cue-ball. Meanwhile, the red will travel a few inches and finish in a pottable position.

Now visualize the pink and black on their respective spots at the end of the game. You have a dead straight pot on the pink and you *need both to win*. Almost without exception, amateurs play this tricky shot slowly, with just sufficient speed to run through on the black. A shot like this is easily missed. If it is, the chances are that your opponent has a simple pot to win the game.

The correct shot to play in this case is sometimes known as a stun run-through – that is, you strike the cue-

thing you can do is to get down, address the centre of the cue-ball and then, suddenly thinking 'I need some side for this shot', point the tip of your cue away from the centre of the cue-ball. If you do this, it means that your cue will not be going straight through the cue-ball but across it.

If you do alter your mind and decide at the last minute to use side, get up, move the whole of your bridge hand and make sure, however much side you are using, that the cue goes straight through the cue-ball without any last second adjustments. One of the best ways to remember this is to imagine the straight line the cue takes when you are hitting straight through the centre of a ball and then make sure that the line the cue takes when you are using side, runs parallel to it.

In Figure 30 there are three reds left, the two near the top cushion not pottable and blocking the path of the black to the one top pocket. The remaining red is easily pottable with the rest, and in doing so the cue-ball will cannon into the two other reds at roughly a half-ball contact.

If this pot is played plain ball, the cue-ball will finish either on, or at best only six centimetres (a couple of inches) away from the side cushion. This is unsatisfactory because one is quite apt to miss the black from this kind of position. Therefore, the pot should be played with right-hand side which will swing the cue-ball off the second object-ball and well clear of the side cushion. The two reds near the top cushion will have been

dislodged into pottable positions and the break should continue for a while without very much difficulty.

In Figure 31, there are five reds left, one of them blocking the path of the pink to the middle pocket, another only two or three centimetres (an inch or so) from the black and blocking its path to the top right-hand pocket. The striker is on a colour and is attempting to cut in the black, a thin shot which would inevitably involve kissing the red near it. There are, however, several ways in which this may be done.

A plain ball pot will involve about a half-ball contact on the nearby red. This will send the red down the table and the cue-ball will finish in the region of the top cushion – end of break! But if you play to pot the black with side, the cue-ball will swing off at a wider angle, contact the red more thinly and knock it via the top cushion into a pottable position as shown. The cue-ball, meanwhile, will travel further because of the thinner contact it has made on the red and come round off top and side cushions into a position where the striker will have a choice of two or three reds.

The shot shown in Figure 34, shows not much difference from the position in which it may be possible to pot the red and hold position on the black by means of a slow screw. Indeed, exactly the same position might call for two different shots simply because of the quality of the cloths – a worn cloth, of course, being less responsive to screw. The chief

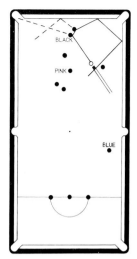

Fig. 31

Fig. 32 **The Swerve:** The position of the balls shows me unable to hit the ball on, the red, by using the cushions. My only means of escape is therefore a swerve round the black, and I raise my bridge and lower my left elbow so that the part of my arm from elbow to wrist helps to keep the bridge stable. I raise the butt of my cue so that I am striking downwards at an angle of about 45°. I strike the cue-ball with strong left-hand side and aim to miss the black by about 15 centimetres (six inches). As the cue-ball passes the black, the spin starts to become effective and the cue-ball should curl round to hit the red.

It is important not to strike the cue-ball too hard. If you do, you will not give the side a chance to take effect.

Fig. 33 **The Masse:** is seldom seen in a snooker match but is mastered by the great billard players as an aid to cannon play, being a concentrated version of the swerve shot. Here I am attempting to pot the black by swerving round the intervening red, and I need to generate so much spin that my cue has to be held almost vertical as it strikes at the left-hand side of the cue-ball. For some reason the shot is easier if one turns one's bridge so that the palm is facing outwards. The cue is almost hitting backwards on to the cue-ball as it makes contact. The shot, played as a firm 'nip', requires a high degree of touch and skill — one for advanced students.

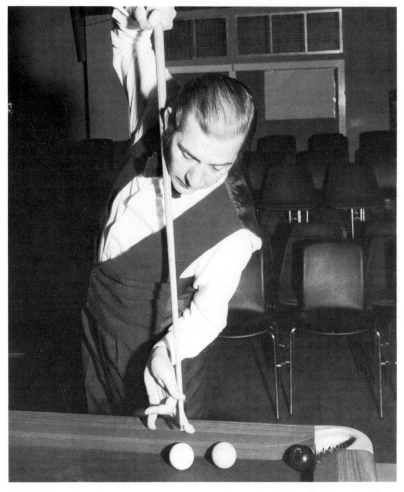

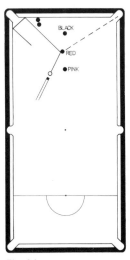

Fig. 34

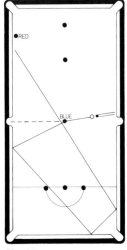

Fig. 35

advantage about using left-hand side in Figure 34 is that by doing so you can be more sure that the cue-ball will not finish near a cushion.

Avoid using side whenever possible but when you are forced into it there are two things you should always remember. Don't get down to address the cue-ball in the centre and then twist the cue to put the side on. If you do this, your cue will not be driven through a straight line from cue-ball to object-ball and you will almost certainly make a mess of whatever shot you are attempting. If you intend to put side on, address the cue-ball with the degree of side you need right at the start.

When using side, grip the cloth firmly with the fingers of your bridge hand and make sure that you continue to do so until you have completed your shot.

I have seen several nervy miscues caused by players moving their bridge hand slightly as they make their shot. If you are playing a plain ball shot this may not result in a miscue but if you are using side, with the tip nearer the edge of the cue-ball, the chances are that it will.

The shot in Figure 35 is a good one to practise. Blue has to be potted very powerfully with plenty of top and left-hand side to swing the cue-ball round off three cushions for position on the last red. As there is not much angle to play with, you have to be sure to get plenty of side on in order to avoid kissing the green.

Some players have a subconscious fear of miscueing when hitting the ball hard with side, and to avoid this hit nearer the centre of the cue-ball than they should. The only way to get out of this tendency is to practise.

Chapter Four
How to Practise

One of the fascinations of snooker is the mixture of technical skill and clear thinking it requires. Player A may have a better cue action, have more screwing ability, or be a better potter but still lose because player B shows better shot selection or better grasp of tactics.

If you have got this far with the book, you have the basic technical equipment in terms of stance and cue action; you have also practised break-building with the black, pink and the smaller colours and by doing so you have made your potting reasonably consistent.

No doubt your cue action, potting and break-building could be improved but I am assuming that as well as practising you are continuing to play competitively in your league and local competitions rather than shutting yourself away for a couple of years striving for perfection on your own.

What you want to know is: how can you make the best use of what ability you have?

Hard practice is undoubtedly top of the list though it is of course a mistake to devote nearly all one's time to practice and only a very small part to play. Solo practice is very intensive and demanding and one's concentration tends to flag after anything much over an hour and a quarter. In addition, the tempo of a game is essentially different from that of practice: in practice, one sets one's own pace, plays all the shots, never feels under the slightest pressure; in a game, one can only play when one's opponent is not playing, can only play from the position in which he leaves one and so on.

In other words, the two dangers of practising too much and playing too little are:

(1) that it is easier to become jaded or stale;

(2) that it is possible to become too self-absorbed and ignore the fact that a game of billiards or snooker re-quires at least two players.

Figure 36, Shot 1, is an exercise designed to promote proficiency round the black spot. There are, of course, a number of variations of this practice position but this one is a particularly good test of ability round the black spot as each red and each black has to be got on just right in order to keep the break going. You will notice as you play this position that as you pot each red another red becomes pottable. A similar kind of thing can often happen in matches and it is something I myself am always on the look-out for.

Figure 36, Shot 2, is a good position for practising break building with the smaller colours. Big breaks cannot be made with the smaller colours alone but an important stage of a big break often takes place in the baulk half of the table. Of course, it is not always big breaks which win matches. It is often that useful 15 or 20 near the end of the game. Some of the shots in this exercise are quite difficult and you will find yourself playing one or two tricky shots with the rest. Keep playing them though – the more you play them, the easier they'll get.

Figures 37 and 38 represent two of the positions I use for practising with the pink and blue. With the positions shown in Figure 37 I always try to pot as many pinks as possible into the middle pocket and, with the position in Figure 38 I always try to pot as many blues as possible into the various corner pockets. In Figure 38, I do not try to play any position when potting the reds except to leave the cue-ball in a part of the table roughly covered by the four circles I have drawn. This exercise, in fact, is mainly potting practice but you will often find that these longish blues are just what you need to keep a break going if you have drifted a bit out of position.

Every practice session should contain some time spent at long straight

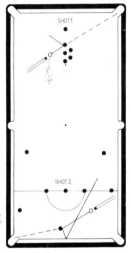

Fig. 36

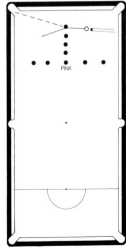

Fig. 37

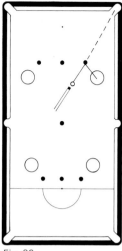

Fig. 38

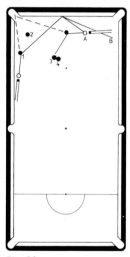

Fig. 39

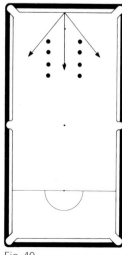

Fig. 40

pots, the best test of straight cueing there is. The better player you become, however, the more time you will tend to spend practising round the black spot, which is, after all, the area in which most big breaks are made.

Obvious though it is, I must emphasize that the first thing a player who wants to make big breaks in this way must do is to pot so many blacks off the spot that he feels absolutely confident of potting the black no matter what the angle or whether he is using stun, screw, side or whatever – but there is more to it than this.

The reason why billiards often seems an easy game is that, with a little control, one can play a series of easy shots. This is the ideal to aim for with snooker. Even though, in a century break, there is almost bound to be at least one pot that is not easy, the vast majority of big breaks are composed primarily of relatively easy pots for there is no player in the world who can keep getting difficult pots shot after shot. The chief skill of break-building is to use one's control to keep playing easy shots.

Of course this is much easier to say than do. In many breaks, ball control or lack of it, has a 'snowballing' effect. For example, in Figure 39, with your first shot, you have potted the red and obtained position on the black. But are you in position A or position B?

You will probably pot the black almost as many times from position B as you would from position A but this is not the main point. From position B you would even be able, quite easily, to get on a red, red no. 2, but even this is not the main point. The correct way to play involves finishing Shot 1 at position A and then potting the black to separate red 3 and 4 while staying in good position on red no. 2.

Now consider the 'snowball' effect of finishing Shot 1 at the inferior position B; after a slightly more difficult black, you can pot red 2 to get back on the black, which is easy in itself but involves getting at a particular angle on it in order to have a chance of disturbing the last two reds. However, even if you do get a suitable angle on the black you are no means certain to kiss the last two reds as you would wish.

Therefore, the full consequences of playing Shot 1 incorrectly are not really shown until you have played three more shots, but if you play the first shot correctly your next seven shots, at least, should be relatively easy. In fact, what I am trying to put over is the not generally realized idea that the effect of an initial good or bad shot 'snowballs'. In other words, one correctly selected and played shot can make a break, just as one incorrectly selected and played shot can bring the break to a premature end.

Figure 40 shows a useful practice position for building a break off the black. Once you get the hang of it you will probably sink eight reds and eight blacks without too much difficulty but it is a very useful position indeed for gaining knowledge of the path the cue-ball takes, having potted the black and bounced off the top cushion. You will notice three arrows in this diagram. These indicate three of the more likely paths the cue-ball will take, having potted the black in attempting to gain a position on a red.

You will notice from the two outer arrows that it is often necessary to skim past a red by quite a narrow margin in order both to gain position on a red and keep away from the side cushion. The greater the margin by which you pass the red on these shots (or the nearer the cue-ball strays to the side cushion) the more my 'snowball' theory comes into operation. From an imperfect position you may be able to pot the red and even another black, but you will find the cue-ball gradually slipping out of position, the break gradually becoming less fluent, until you soon break down.

When you have got the hang of this position you can try a more difficult variation of it. This is indicated by the centre arrow in Figure 40. When you have potted a black, try to use this central avenue as much as possible. The rest of your control here, of course, is getting the cue-ball as much on the line formed by the pink and black spots as possible. As long as you can keep the cue-ball going along this line then your break ought to proceed quite happily but, as soon as you let the cue-ball stray too near one or other of the two lines of reds, then you can expect trouble. In certain cases, even when you finish very close to a ball, you may still be able to pot it but anything much in the way of cue-ball control, such as follow-through or screw, is usually either difficult or impossible. Similarly, if you finish very near a ball in one of the lines, you may still be able, by cueing over an intervening ball, to pot a ball from the other line, but here again, even though you may get the pot itself, you will very likely begin to lose position.

Many players are a little contemptuous of practice positions like this. 'You never get them in a game so why practise them?' they ask. Well, a concert pianist never plays a series of scales and exercises at a concert, so why does he practise them?

The answer is obvious, of course. He practises in this way because of the discipline and technical mastery he thereby acquires. Another thing I have found (and I expect most concert pianists find it too) is that, after I have been slogging away at quite a difficult practise position, the game itself seems so much more fun and in some cases, very much easier! Finally, if you keep practising one particular position you will be able to measure your improvement by the bigger breaks you make from it. It is hard work, I know, but it is worth it in the end!

Ted Lowe, whose commentaries are still to be heard on *Pot Black* and other televised snooker, had a habit of saying when Joe Davis was shaping up to pot a black: 'And now Joe's on his favourite ball, the black.'

Well, Joe is not the only one who likes potting the black but there are times when the break has to be built up in another way.

The blue seemed to me to be worth some detailed treatment because it is often a 'recovery' ball: when position has been lost or not yet obtained round the black spot, the blue can often offer a means of keeping the break going. When one is the 'right' side of the blue, that is nearer the baulk cushion than the top, and there are a few reds 'open' round the pink and black spots, the position is straightforward enough not to need any comment from me. Therefore the

only diagram I have drawn in which the cue-ball is the 'right' side of the blue (Figure 41) is one in which, failing a possibility of playing position on a particular red, it is necessary to crash the cue-ball into the pack.

However, there is more than one way to do this. By using stun and perhaps some left-hand side, it is possible to hit the pack without using the cushions. Alternatively, the shot could be played with top and left-hand side, thus swinging the cue-ball into the pack off two cushions.

In this case, the second method has a greater chance of leaving a good position. You will notice that the reds near the pink are packed more tightly together than those at the rear of the pack. There is far more chance of leaving a good position by coming into a fairly 'loose' pack obliquely than going into a very tight pack frontally. Apart from anything else, there is always a danger of going into a 'tight' pack full on and leaving the cue-ball touching the first red contacted.

The main thing to remember is this: when you have to split the pack don't think that one method is as good as another. Try to contact the pack at a point where there is most chance of shaking out a few pottable reds. Whenever you can, try to go into the pack at a point where there is a slight space between each red, but if you must go into a tightly jammed pack, try to contact the first object-ball at a slight angle. This will reduce the danger of leaving the cue-ball touching a red.

Incidentally, it is not a good idea to go into the pack when the reds are still roughly in a triangle, as the cue-ball tends to glance off either into or near a top pocket.

My other two diagrams refer to situations in which the cue-ball is the 'wrong' side of the blue. In Figure 42, for instance, there are a few reds open in the region of the pink and black spots, and to get the cue-ball into a position to pot them it is necessary for it to travel in and out of baulk. In this particular position a plain ball shot will result in the cue-ball cannoning on to the yellow, so stun and right-hand side have to be employed of course; too much stun and side is as

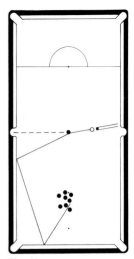

Fig. 41

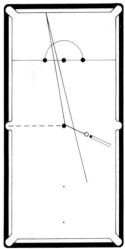

Fig. 42

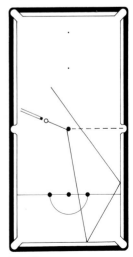

Fig. 43

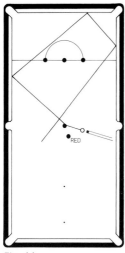

Fig. 44

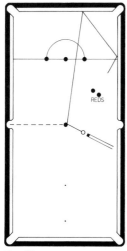

Fig. 45

Fig. 46

bad as too little since the cue-ball has not only to cross the baulk line between yellow and brown but re-crosses it at roughly the same point. The best way to do this is to aim to miss the yellow by about eight to ten centimetres (three to four inches). If you have enough side on, the cue-ball should return up the table on roughly the same line as it went down.

Some players prefer to do without side in this position, on the grounds that it is difficult enough to get between yellow and brown in the first place without trying to get back again. However, if one does not use side, the cue-ball will very likely finish near the side cushion and thus lead to a none too easy next shot. The correct positional shot is slightly the harder of the two but it is the one that must be played.

Sometimes, as in Figure 43, it is necessary to use running (left-hand) side either for positional considerations or because it is too difficult to get the cue-ball to avoid other balls in returning up the table. It often seems a bit unnatural to use left-hand side for a pot like this, and for this reason the shot is often missed. The only cure for this feeling is to practise the shot until it no longer seems unfamiliar.

In Figure 44 you are on the blue the wrong side and there is one red left. In this type of position it is often possible for the cue-ball to travel in and out of baulk between the yellow and brown but if it is necessary to hit the blue fairly full to pot it, you may find that the best way to get position on the red is to pot the blue at speed and, making sure that you have struck the cue-ball well above centre, use the cushions as indicated in the diagram. Depending on the exact position of the ball, you may find it an advantage to use running side to help

swing the cue-ball round the cushions.

Be careful about this, though, as it is only too easy to use too much side and thus swing the cue-ball into an unwanted cannon on the green. Of course, if the brown and green spots are unoccupied, you may be able to use this type of shot more often. It is, in fact, quite easy to execute, provided that you make quite sure that you strike the cue-ball well above the centre and, as with all powerful shots, you keep your head down and your body still.

Figure 45 shows a variation of the 'in and out of baulk' shot in that, after potting the blue, the cue-ball travels between the green and brown instead of the yellow and brown. In Figure 45 there are two reds left. They are so situated that either is pottable into the one middle pocket but neither is pottable into the other. The cue-ball is too far from the blue, and at too much of an angle for you to be able to get position on the reds by means of a slow screw. However, by using screw and right-hand side, it is possible to go between the green and brown on the way into baulk, and between green and side cushion on the way out. One of the main dangers with this shot, of course, is colliding with the green.

Finally Figure 46 is a practice position designed to improve your potting and control of the blue ball. It shows eight reds in various parts of the table and the blue on its spot. The idea here is simply to pot eight reds and eight blues. Most players when they practise break-building do so almost exclusively round the black spot. That, of course, is where most breaks are made but there are times when the pink and black are safe and you are only too glad to run up twenty or so with reds and blues.

26

Chapter Five
Needing the Lot to Win

In competitive snooker a large proportion of frames are decided either at the colours stage or with only one or two reds remaining. A mathematical reason enters into this, of course, as at no other time in the game is the consecutive potting of six balls worth as many as 27 points or the consecutive potting of eight balls possibly worth 35 points. Often, when a player needs all the remaining balls to win, the key shot is gaining position on the yellow, having potted the last red and a colour.

Many players try to make sure that they are in position on one of the baulk colours, yellow, green or brown after the last red so that the cue-ball will not have far to travel to be in position on the yellow preparatory to clearing the colours. However, this policy is often needlessly over-cautious and can in any case misfire. In short, it is not necessarily the easiest and therefore safest way of clearing the table.

Figures 47 and 48 show different ways of potting the black and gaining position on the yellow. I know that at this point many players reading this book will say – 'It all looks easy enough on paper but it's ten times as hard on the table.'

In other words, these players lack confidence in their own ability! Unless they do something about it, this will always be so. What, in fact, I do advise them to do is to practise these shots until they can play them properly. If you have played a shot regularly in practice you cannot help but be more confident when you come to play a similar shot in a match.

The shot in Figure 47 is rarely attempted by many players *because they lack the confidence* which practice and a thorough knowledge of angles gives. Position on the yellow is obtained by playing plain ball (or with a little right-hand side if necessary) and making the cue-ball bounce off the two side cushions, as indicated. Most players fear the in-off in the

centre pocket, though only because they have not practised enough. One word of warning: don't be too ready to use right-hand side as a collision with the blue will almost certainly spell disaster, either in the shape of an in-off, a snooker, or lost position.

Often the merest fraction will decide you to play one shot in preference to another. The shots in Figure 48 are a case in point. In a diagram it is impossible to indicate the minute differences in position, so, for the sake of clarity and simplicity, I have shown shots A and B with the cue-ball, at the beginning of a shot in the same position for both.

However, for A I want you to imagine that the cue-ball is a shade nearer the top of the cushion than it is for B. In other words the black must be potted about half-ball in Figure 47, between half and three-quarter ball in Figure 48, Shot A, and about three-quarter ball in Figure 48, Shot B.

Figure 48A is probably the most difficult of the three. It is played with screw and right-hand side. You will notice from the diagram that the cue-ball's path is curved. The reason for this is that the impact of screw and right-hand side makes the cue-ball spring sharply from the black, though after a while the side, travelling against the nap, causes the cue-ball to straighten up.

The main dangers with this shot are screwing too fiercely and having the cue-ball finish on or near the side cushion, or not screwing enough and kissing the pink. Some people think that the difficulty of the shot is increased with the use of side. In fact, however, you have very much less chance of gaining a good position without the use of side because the cue-ball's course will continue on a straight line and will not 'bend' into position as it would if side was used.

Figure 48, Shot B provides, apart from anything else, a really good test of cueing. As the angle is slightly

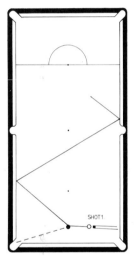

Fig. 47

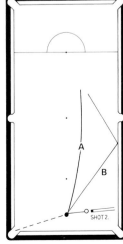

Fig. 48

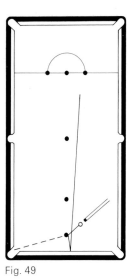

Fig. 49

straighter than in 48A another way of obtaining position on the yellow has to be sought for. The correct shot to play is a strong screw back with strong left-hand side. The latter will cause the cue-ball to spin strongly off the side cushion and ensure that the pot of the yellow should not have to be attempted from too great a distance.

With this shot you must make sure that the cue-ball is struck low enough and with enough side. On all strong shots everyone has an inbred tendency to lift his head. After playing the game for some years you may think you have eliminated this fault. So you may have done for most shots – but with this particular shot make a conscious effort, as I do, to keep your head still. Even so, this is still not an easy shot and on a very slow table with dead cushions, it may be impossible. In general, though, you will find this a very useful shot to acquire as it can be useful to you in countless different situations.

The top cushion can be employed for two other standard ways of getting from last black on to the yellow. Figure 49 shows a half-ball black played with just a touch of left-hand side so that the cue-ball finishes, if your judgement of strength is accurate, on a half or three-quarter ball yellow. If the cue-ball is slightly to the right of left of its original position as shown in the diagram you will need either more or less side. When you are assessing the amount you will need, make sure primarily that the cue-ball is going to miss the pink on its journey down the table but also be careful that you do not use too much side so that the cue-ball is pulled towards the side cushion.

For this reason, if I have a choice, I prefer the shot in Figure 50 which uses not only the top but the side cushion. This is played with stun and left-hand side so that, after coming off two cushions, the cue-ball is moving towards the yellow rather than, as in Figure 49, edging away from it. Very often, of course, I do have a choice in that I am usually able to pot the last red in such a way that I leave myself the cue-ball at a desirable angle on the black. As these diagrams show, there is a fair range of

choice but avoid like the plague leaving yourself straight on the black.

It is possible (see Figure 51) to gain position on the yellow by screwing back fiercely with left-hand side so that the cue-ball spins sharply off the cushion but this is a top professional class shot which even top professionals prefer not to have to play. Whenever I leave myself straight on the last black to get on the yellow I consider that I have played a bad shot.

My own pet way of getting from black to yellow is none of these but a shot from the other side of the black, Shot 1 in Figure 52. In this particular shot a plain half-ball shot will not do because the cue-ball will be left too far from the yellow. The correct thing to do here is to play a stun shot which will widen the angle of 'throw' off the black and bring the cue-ball into a better position on the yellow. With this shot some players are afraid of an in-off in the middle pocket. This, of course, can happen if you badly misjudge the amount of stun needed but unless you are very careless there is ample margin of error.

The most frequent way in which the pot is missed is for the black to strike the top cushion. This happens when the player is too anxious to get down the table for the yellow. Therefore, as always, make absolutely sure of the pot. If you don't do this, you won't have another shot that break anyway.

Do not use side for this shot. If you do use any left-hand side, it is quite likely that the cue-ball will slide off the cushion and finish behind the baulk line.

In Figure 52, Shot 2, however, a little left-hand side is often an advantage, depending of course on the exact position of the cue-ball. As shown in the diagram, the cue-ball travels into position on the yellow via both top and side cushions. It goes without saying of course that you should not use side unless it is necessary as any pot is made more difficult if side is used. If, however, side is necessary (if you think for instance, that the cue-ball will go dangerously near the middle pocket without it) then remember that you will not need to hit the cue-ball quite so hard, as the

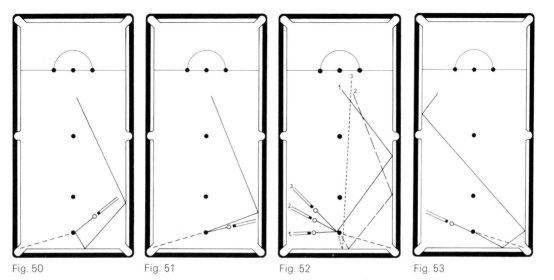

Fig. 50   Fig. 51   Fig. 52   Fig. 53

side will do some of the work for you.

Be sure though that you have it quite clear in your mind what you are attempting before you address the cue-ball. Then, if you are going to use side, place your bridge hand on the table accordingly. Do not place your bridge hand for a plain-ball shot and then try to apply side obliquely. This, I know, sounds elementary but it is surprising how many players fall into this simple error.

Figure 52, Shot 3 shows a way of obtaining position on the yellow without using the side cushion. This shot may come in useful when some of the colours are not on their spots but prevent the cue-ball from travelling off two cushions towards the yellow. With this shot, of course, it is vital not to kiss the pink. However, for positional reasons, it is also vital that the cue-ball should not miss the pink by too much. In fact, the smaller this margin is, the better, because as you will notice from the angle of the shot, it is inevitable that the farther the cue-ball travels down the table the more it drifts over to the left-hand side of the table (looking from baulk). Unless you are careful the cue-ball will finish too near the side cushion for comfort but, once you are used to the shot, there is no need for this to happen.

You could call this shot an extended version of one which is frequently played round the black spot when there are still some reds re-

maining. It may well be that the path to the pottable red you have selected on which to play position, has been narrowed through the awkward position of another ball or balls. Here again, if you have the confidence and judgement to pot the black, skim past the pink and obtain perfect position on the red you have selected, you can well get in with a useful or even match-winning break which you would otherwise perhaps never have made.

Sometimes, either through bad luck or, more often, bad judgement, none of these shots is any use. Take, for example, Figure 53 where the cue-ball is almost straight on the black. The only thing to do here is to pot the black at speed and, using left-hand side, come across the face of the pink, strike the cushion just below the middle pocket, and take the yellow across the table into the baulk pocket. It is possible to go in-off in the middle so that amount of side has to be judged to a very fine margin.

Perhaps the worst position of all (short of being tight under the side cushion) is being straight on the black from the same side of the table. For a professional all is not quite lost as a tremendously powerful screw back with right-hand side (more power than is needed for Figure 51 for instance) can take the cue-ball spinning off the side cushion and down past the blue for position on the yellow. Once you can play this shot

29

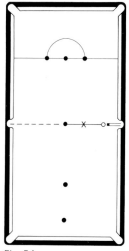

Fig. 54

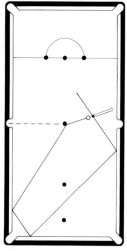

Fig. 55

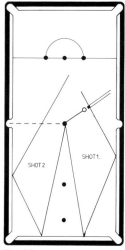

SHOT 1.

SHOT 2

Fig. 56

you should think about writing a book yourself. In fact, this was the shot I had to play after the fifteenth red in my world record break of 147 in Capetown in 1965.

On many occasions, of course, it will not be practicable to take the black with your last red so I shall conclude this section with three positions involving the blue, each of which presupposes that you have tried to get on the correct side of the blue (that is about five centimetres [two inches] nearer the top cushion than the baulk cushion) but have, in fact, left the cue-ball either straight on the blue or just that little bit the wrong side.

In Figure 54, you have left yourself straight on the blue so that the only way you can get on the yellow is by screwing back along the line drawn from the blue to the middle pocket. When you do so, however, it is important to have in your mind exactly where you want the cue-ball to finish.

Some players would try to leave a straight yellow with a view to screwing back straight for the green. They would be better advised to screw the cue-ball back to a point which leaves them a natural three-quarter ball pot of the yellow and a natural in and out of baulk shot to get on the green as shown. In Figure 55, the cue-ball has run eight or ten centimetres (three or four inches) the 'wrong' side of the blue. You might possibly consider taking the yellow and then taking the yellow again. However, we will as-

sume that you need a blue to win the frame – though whether I needed the blue or not I would probably still take it in preference to the yellow in this position. Play to pot the blue at speed with top and left-hand side. The cue-ball should then come off the side and top cushions, pass between the pink and black, hit the opposite side cushion by the middle pocket and finish in good position on the yellow.

Figure 56 shows two ways of potting the blue to get position on the yellow when the cue-ball has gone eight or ten centimetres (three or four inches) nearer baulk than it has in the position shown in Figure 55.

In Figure 56, Shot 1, position on the yellow is achieved by potting the blue with power and some screw and left-hand side. Be careful not to use too much screw, for this will not only tend to reduce the run of the cue-ball but also, if the cue-ball strikes the top cushion too near the top pocket, land you somewhere by the blue and not in very good position on the yellow.

Shot 1 in Figure 56 is a much surer way of getting on the yellow than is Shot 2, but you may be forced to play the latter if, for instance, there is another ball which has strayed off its spot to stop you playing Shot 1.

In Shot 2 you play with stun and right-hand side to bring the cue-ball off the top and side cushion as shown. The big snag about this way of getting on the yellow is that your weight has to be nearly perfect. A few centimetres or inches too short or too long and you have no position at all.

Chapter Six
Playing with Margin for Error

One important principle of positional play which has been implicit in much of what I have written so far is the desirability of leaving yourself with maximum margin of error in positional play. It was, if you remember, the reason why I preferred the shot in Figure 50 to the one in Figure 49.

It now seems time to clarify this principle so in Figure 57 we will assume that the black is the only colour on which it is possible to obtain position. However, there are three reds clustered round it in such a way that the cue-ball must finish at a certain angle to the black in order for the pot to be 'on'. There are two reds 'in the open' as shown (A and B), both fairly easy.

The correct red to take is, of course, the one I have labelled A, for the cue-ball after potting the red, must bounce off the cushion and proceed naturally along the line on which the cue-ball must finish for the black to be pottable. If one takes the red labelled 'B' it is possible to obtain position on the black but the margin of error is very small.

If red 'B' is taken, the cue-ball comes off the top cushion, across the potting line. In other words, the speed of the cue-ball must be gauged into eight or ten centimetres (three or four inches) whereas, if red 'A' is taken, the speed of the cue-ball can vary by more than 60 centimetres (two feet)!

The principle illustrated by this position is: **never play across a line to gain position when one can play along it.**

In Figure 58 the striker is on the blue and there is one 'open' red in the small cluster round the pink spot on which he can comfortably gain position. The correct way to play Shot 'A' is to pot blue and bounce naturally off the cushion as shown. By playing this way, there is a margin of, at least, 60 centimetres (two feet) in the

matter of positioning the cue-ball perfectly for the 'open' red.

Some players might choose to use stun to gain position instead of using the cushion. I have inserted this stroke in Figure 58 as well (Shot 'B'), and indicated the points between which the cue-ball must finish in order to retain perfect position. As can be seen, the margin of error is about 15 to 20 centimetres (six to eight inches) – even assuming the correct amount of stun is used.

Sometimes, of course, one is forced into using this shot – if, for example, an intervening ball prevents one from using the cushion – and there is, in fact, enough margin of error to make the shot feasible. Nevertheless, if the shot is 'on', the advantage of using the cushion in this position is obvious.

In Figure 59 the striker is on the yellow and there is one open red marked 'X' in a cluster near the pink. Most players would play the shot I have marked 'A', using only one cushion and leaving a margin of error of about 30 centimetres (one foot). Any professional, I am sure, would use two cushions when playing this shot because this is yet another instance of the preferability of 'coming into' a shot rather than 'going across' it.

For the correct shot, which I have marked 'B', one needs less screw and left-hand side than one needs for shot 'A'. I know that some players prefer using either a lot of screw or none at all and find control difficult when they have to use a 'medium' amount. However, this is one thing that simply has to be worked on if you wish to improve your technique.

Another aspect of giving yourself maximum margin of error whilst still retaining a positive approach to the game occurs when you are in the situation when almost all the open reds have been potted.

In Figure 60, both shots involve

Opposite below:
Cliff Thorburn, 1980 World Champion from Canada.

Fig. 57

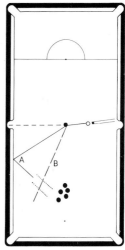

Fig. 58

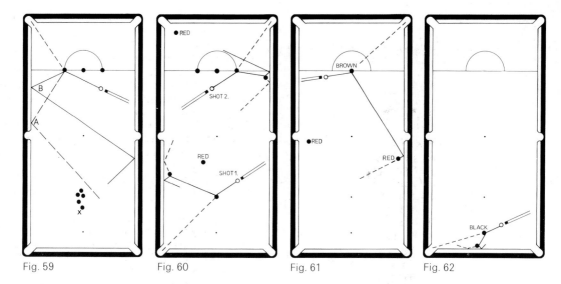

Fig. 59   Fig. 60   Fig. 61   Fig. 62

thinking several moves ahead and making use of the type of knowledge most easily acquired through billiards. In Shot 1, most players would concentrate on getting on the red in the open, taking another blue or pink and then thinking out what to do with the red that is 'safe'.

The correct shot is to pot the pink and cannon on to the 'safe' red about half-ball making it pottable in the middle pocket either next shot or when one has taken the other red and a colour.

It is important to know on which part of the 'safe' red one is making the cannon. Contact the red too thinly and it may not be moved into a pottable position. Contact it nearly full in the face and the same applies, though, of course, in both cases one would still be handily placed for the open red.

Figure 60, Shot 2 also includes a cannon. Most players might take the brown on the grounds that they are unlikely to pot the last red and that, therefore, taking the green would mean one less point than necessary. Providing that you have the knowledge to make you confident of hitting the correct side of the 'safe' red, as shown, taking the green will almost certainly pave the way for you to take both remaining reds.

With my shot in Figure 61, most players would take the brown and simply make sure of being able to pot the red near the middle pocket. The

correct shot, as shown, is a screw to get behind the red which is near the cushion. One can then pot the red over the middle pocket, leave oneself on the 'baulk' side of the blue and go up the table for the remaining red which, by now, should be somewhere near the pink spot.

The lesson to learn here is to keep on the look out for a chance to nudge an awkward red into a pottable position in such a way that you retain position on a red that is already pottable.

One decision which has to be made quite frequently is whether to play position on a ball lying on or near a cushion, or to try and knock it into a better position. Figure 62 is a good example of this. On a table with easy or nicely undercut pockets, the correct shot is to stun in the black and leave a nice angle on the red along the cushion. On a table with difficult pockets, one should run-through the black and try to nudge red into a better position, as I have shown.

Sometimes though, the choice does not depend solely on how easy the pockets are. A pot along the cushions at a vital stage of a match is a very different proposition to the same pot in a friendly game with nothing at stake. If, say, one is 20 in front in the deciding frame of an Amateur Championship match it will usually pay to pot the black and try to knock the red into an easy position. If you succeed, that's fine – you pot the red and another black and you've virtually won. If you don't, you can still put your opponent in trouble with a safety shot. On the other hand, a slot pot along the cushion is all right if you get it. If you don't and leave the red in the jaws, you have virtually presented your opponent with the game.

Figure 63 is another position where one should play to nudge the red into a better position. I have shown how the shot would work out if played perfectly but it is always a good thing when playing this type of shot to have some sort of alternative in one's mind if it does not work out. In this case, if one fails to complete the cannon successfully, there is another red on the opposite side cushion which is doubleable.

If one has to play this double make sure, if the game is close, that the cue-ball finishes near the baulk cushion. If one misses the double the red is almost certain to go safe. If one gets it, one can either pot one of the baulk colours, or, if the cue-ball is too close to the baulk cushion, trickle up behind one of them.

In a match, the main object is to win: big breaks are of only secondary importance. In a big match there is generally quite a lot of safety play with the result that some balls inevitably get knocked under the cushion. Furthermore, it is often policy, when you have made a 30 break or so, to leave your opponent in a safe position rather than take the risk of splitting a cluster of otherwise impossible reds or of knocking a ball out from under the cushion. In a practice game, of course, the result is of less – often, indeed, of no – importance and consequently, with not much safety play and not much tension, big breaks are more frequent.

In a championship match there is much to be said for playing within your limitations, taking the loose balls, and then closing the game up. It is absolutely senseless to go for a spectacular odds-against shot when you can, for certain, leave your opponent in such a position that he has got to play a very good shot to avoid leaving you 'in' again.

There is no point in giving away half of what you have acquired by attempting to do too much. But we

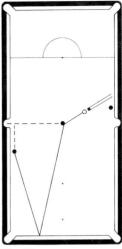

Fig. 63

mustn't lose our sense of proportion. There are times when there is such a good chance to split the pack profitably that it is wrong to pass it up. By splitting the pack at the right time you can compile a winning break, whereas if you play safe, your opponent still has a chance (in some cases, admittedly, a very slight one) to get back in the game if he produces his best form. In other words, whether or not to split the pack depends on the precise position of the balls and on the state of one's confidence.

In Figure 64, Shot 1, for example, the black is not at all easy, it is a hard enough shot merely to pot it without attempting to screw into the pack. Even if you pot the black and hit the pack it is not certain that the balls will split at all favourably. However, if you pot the black plain ball you are bound to finish in a position which will give you an excellent chance of putting the cue-ball under the baulk cushion next shot, Shot 2. On the other hand, should you miss the black in attempting to screw into the pack (as is quite possible even for a top player) there is a good chance that you will leave your opponent an opening.

In Figure 65, however, you *must* attempt to split the pack. The first thing to remember when you realize that a cluster of reds has to be opened out, is to get in a suitable position to do so. In the position in the diagram, for instance, it is worse than useless to get dead straight or even nearly straight on the black as it then becomes impossible both to pot the black and cannon into the reds. It is, of course, possible to crash into the reds good and hard and trust to luck as regards position. Indeed, there are occasions when this is the only thing you can do. But in the majority of positions you stand more chance of splitting the pack successfully if you think beforehand what part of the pack you are going to hit and what is likely to happen to the reds afterwards.

In this particular case, if you aim for the point indicated in the diagram (which means that two reds will be hit almost simultaneously) it is very likely that all the reds will be knocked into pottable positions. You will, in

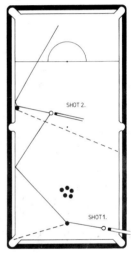

Fig. 64

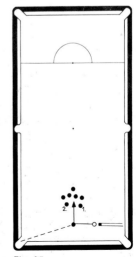

Fig. 65

33

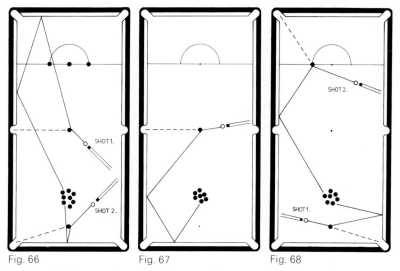

Fig. 66   Fig. 67   Fig. 68

any case, be in a good position to pot either red no. 1 or red no. 2. Be sure, however, to get enough screw on for this shot. If you don't do this, you may contact red no. 2 full and consequently not finish in a very favourable position.

A sensible general rule to follow is: the more difficult the pot, the more reluctant you should be to split the pack. But don't fall into the opposite trap of excessive caution – for the most successful players, at the end of the day, are those who have not only taken their chances but have also created some.

There are several ways to smash the pack, some of which are more likely than others to leave good position. But whichever method you use, a bit of luck always comes in handy.

In Figure 66, Shot 1, for instance, it takes quite a good shot even to make contact with the pack. When potting the blue and coming in and out of baulk, the more usual way to get back up the table is with screw and right-hand side which gets the cue-ball in and out of baulk between the yellow and the brown.

For some reason which I have never quite been able to fathom, it is easier to pot the blue with screw and **right**-hand side than with screw and left-hand side. On occasions like this, however, you have to force yourself to play the shot the 'unnatural' way, using enough screw to miss the yellow and enough left-hand side to swing the cue-ball off the baulk and

side cushions as shown.

Figure 66, Shot 2 shows my favourite pack-opening shot, the secret of which lies wholly in leaving a nice half-ball angle on the black.

Another way in which the pack can often be smashed is by a vigorous pot off the blue. To do this, however, you need a reasonably wide angle on the blue in order to ensure that the cue-ball will be travelling fairly fast when it goes into the pack. If you leave yourself fairly straight on the blue and try to stun into the pack, most of the speed will have left the cue-ball by the time it makes contact with the reds.

Figure 67 shows the shot to play when you have left yourself with too straight a blue. If you pot the blue at speed with no side, the cue-ball will go nowhere near the pack of reds. Therefore, play this pot with plenty of top and left-hand side. This should swing the cue-ball into the pack with a reasonable chance of leaving a red or two in a pottable position.

In Figure 68, Shot 1, it is possible to make contact with the pack of reds with a stun shot. Here again, though, most of the speed will have left the cue-ball by the time it hits the reds. Therefore, the correct shot to play is a powerful run-through, potting the black into the corner pocket and bringing the cue-ball into the pack via the side cushion. When the black is nearly straight, you may need left-hand side to bring the cue-ball into the reds, a harder shot certainly, but

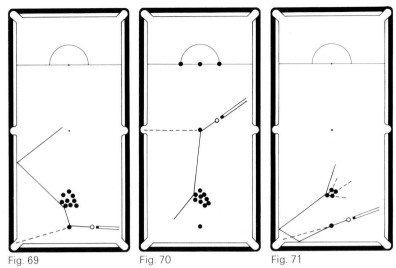

Fig. 69   Fig. 70   Fig. 71

one which sometimes has to be played.

Figure 68, Shot 2, shows the orthodox pack-smashing shot off the yellow, or, if you put the cue-ball in the corresponding place on the other side of the table, off the green. The shot in the diagram needs screw and left-hand side but only a few practice shots will tell you exactly how much.

Figure 69 shows one of those easy looking but all-too-missable shots where you have to pot the black into a 'blind' pocket and screw into the pack. The shot has to be played at speed and, therefore, on the tables where the pockets are not properly undercut, there is some danger of wobbling the black in the jaws and scattering the reds for your opponent.

However, on almost any table, it is still a shot you should go for. I play this kind of shot with screw and right-hand side. Depending on the exact grouping of the reds in the pack, there are two ways I might play this shot. I might screw into the middle of the pack or I might, as shown in the diagram, screw on to the edge of the pack so that the cue-ball can reach the side cushion and, as a result of the side still on it, zip off the side cushion down the table, thus increasing the chances of some fairly easy straightish reds into the corner pocket.

One shot to avoid is one which many amateurs favour; that is, a direct screw from the blue into the pack of reds, as in Figure 70. My objection to this is that if the reds are still in a triangular formation, the cue-ball is likely to slide off them and finish either in or near the corner pocket.

Some amateurs, even when this happens four times out of five, persist in thinking that the balls are running unkindly for them whereas, in fact, the percentages are against them. They would be far better advised to leave a slightly different angle on the blue with their previous shot so that, as in Figure 67, they can use two cushions to split the pack from behind.

There are a number of other rare variations of pack-opening shots, one of which once helped me to make a break of 145 (see Figure 71). I was on 87 and about to take the black. There were three reds left in a group by the pink, none of them pottable. By potting the black plain ball and coming off the top and side cushions I would have missed a cluster of balls (and a chance to knock them into a pottable position) by a wide margin. I therefore played the shot with as much left-hand side as I could possibly cram on, and this sufficiently narrowed the angle at which the cue-ball left the cushions for the cue-ball to clip one of the reds as shown, and knock another red into a pottable position. Apart from this, the other two reds came into pottable positions and I was able to go on and clear the table.

Chapter Seven
Safety Play

There are two kinds of safety play – aggressive and negative. The first is when, without attempting a pot, you actively try to put your opponent in a difficult position. The second is when you merely prevent your opponent from scoring without in any way seizing the initiative – which is often just another way of saying that you are giving the initiative away.

Take safety shots with the first shot of the frame. Some amateurs, though decreasingly few now, actually start the frame by rolling up to the reds. Perfectly safe, of course, but your opponent can simply play gently away from the reds and leave the cue-ball on the bottom cushion.

No, start the frame with either the shot shown in Figure 72 or the one in Figure 73. In Figure 72 strike the cue-ball with right-hand side, contacting the outside red just over quarter-ball so that the cue-ball runs off three cushions to finish on the baulk cushion behind the green. With this contact only the two end reds of the back row will be much disturbed and even these should finish in relatively safe positions, especially if you have gauged the speed of the cue-ball well enough to leave it within an inch or so of the baulk cushion. If so, you have achieved the minimum object of an agressive safety shot: that is, you have left your opponent worse placed than you yourself were.

Figure 73 may look more or less the same shot as Figure 72 and in so far as you use right-hand side and bring the cue-ball back off three cushions to the same place as it finishes in Figure 72, it is.

The difference lies in contacting the second red (not the outside) so that the pack is disturbed much more. There is thus more risk than in Figure 72 that your opponent will have an immediate chance, if he is a good long potter, to pot a long red and get in first.

One of the perennial dilemmas of a snooker player is striking the right balance between attack and defence or 'when to have a go' not only in the early stages of a game but at any stage. It is an inexhaustible problem and, in general, one should follow the sound business principles of weighing risk against potential gain.

It is hardly ever worth taking a big risk for a small gain; a dodgy business to take a big risk for a big gain; much more attractive to take a small risk for a big gain. On the other hand, with the reds well dispersed your opponent may either miss a pot or mishit a safety shot and give you the first chance.

On strange tables or if the match is close, it may pay you to hit the end red (Figure 72); if you are confident, or if you are a frame or so in front or if you can sense your opponent cracking, be readier to hit the second red (Figure 73).

After this initial shot, the opening exchanges of a frame usually settle down to thin safety shots, returning the cue-ball off the side of the pack or one of the loose reds to (as near as possible) the baulk cushion.

Be on the lookout, right from the start, for the 'shot to nothing', that is, a chance to pot with no great risk of leaving your opponent a chance if you miss. There are countless examples of this but I will content myself with one of the most common (see Figure 74). Here, the quarter-ball pot can be attempted secure in the knowledge you are also playing a safety shot, for the other reds and the green and blue will almost certainly prevent your opponent from potting this red even if it wobbles in the pocket or stays near it.

If the shot is successful, two possibilities exist. One is that the cue-ball will stop as indicated to give you a chance to pot the green in the middle and travel up the table for one of the loose reds and, you hope, a useful break. The second is that the cue-ball may stop on or very near the baulk cushion, thus making any attempt to pot either green or brown very risky.

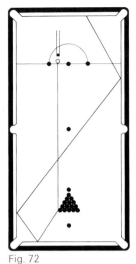
Fig. 72

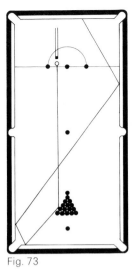
Fig. 73

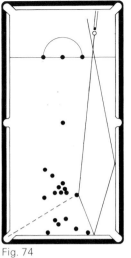
Fig. 74

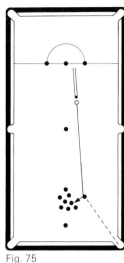
Fig. 75

In this case, you would simply roll the cue-ball up behind the green as gently as possible, not only leaving your opponent snookered but with a real risk of leaving you an opening.

It pays to concentrate on these shots to nothing. There is a tendency, particularly if your concentration is not what it should be, to try only half-heartedly to pot these shot to nothing reds. 'Well, I can't leave much even if I miss it,' is the sort of thought you have.

This is negative thinking. Think of shots like this as either a chance to start a break or a chance to put your opponent in trouble. Don't wait for your opponent to make mistakes. Go out to win yourself or put him under so much pressure that he has to make mistakes.

One of the ideals I have set myself as a professional is to cut chance and luck out of my game as much as possible. Of course, this can never be done completely but it is an ideal to aim at, and many players do aim at it. I think that, given equal ability, a player like this will do better, in the long run, than what I call an 'inspirational' player who really goes for his shots and hopes that the balls will go safe if he misses one. It is in some ways harder to play this latter type of player, for nothing is more disconcerting than to see him get an outrageous pot which he should never have gone for, or, perhaps even worse, miss the pot, scatter the balls

in all directions and leave you dead safe!

Figure 75 is the sort of shot I mean. The striker has a half-ball pot red on in the top left-hand pocket. If he gets it, the position is uncertain, if he misses it the chances are that he will leave a good opening for his opponent. Yet I once saw a very distinguished amateur play this shot in a match, get it, somehow or other finish on the black and make a 30-odd break.

When I suggested after the game that it was rather a daring shot to play, I was told 'Oh, I don't know. If that red had been the only ball on the table, you wouldn't have thought twice about going for it. Why get frightened because there are a few other balls about?' You can admire the confidence if not the soundness of this philosophy.

Yet there are times when one has to 'have a go'. Figure 76 can be one of them **if you are about 40 or 50 behind.** In this case, it is vital to pot all or most of the remaining reds with big value colours, if one is to win the game. As the position stands, all the reds are pottable and there is an excellent chance of a good break if the first red can be potted.

It is not a good policy to play a safety shot or two in the hope that a more certain red will materialize as by this time two or three reds will probably have been knocked safe, thus spoiling the chance of a break;

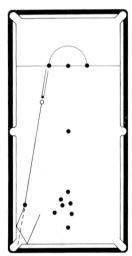
Fig. 76

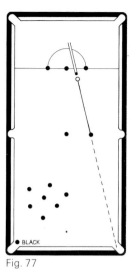

Fig. 77

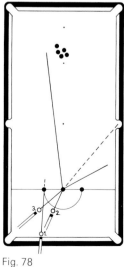

Fig. 78

however, if you are 40 or so in front instead of behind it is not a bad idea to play a few safety shots with this very end in view. On many occasions I have seen frames lost through a player overplaying his hand because of a deceptively big lead.

Figure 77, however, is an instance when the player ought to go for a pot regardless of the score. The cue-ball is just short of the baulk line and there are seven reds left, six in the top right hand corner, one almost on a line from the blue spot to the middle pocket. Pink is on its spot.

The correct shot is to try to stun in the isolated red, to leave a slight angle on the blue so that it can then be potted and the cue-ball positioned in a break-building position. If the first red is potted, a good break should follow. If it isn't, the red (unless the attempt at the pot is a very wild one) should wobble in the jaws and run safe. As long as the cue-ball is stunned dead, none of the remaining reds is pottable.

One of the subtler 'attack or defence?' dilemmas is posed by Figure 78 which shows the type of position in which many players never quite know when to snooker and when to attempt to build a break.

In Figure 78, Position 1, you have potted a red and finished very near the baulk cushion. Your alternatives are to pot the brown or to trickle up behind the green thus leaving your opponent snookered. Which alternative you choose depends, of course, on the position of the reds. The pot brown is no certainty by anyone's standards so if there were any reds which were pottable into either of the middle or top pockets, I would choose the other alternative of trickling up as closely behind the green as I could.

However, if all the other reds were in a safe position, closely locked together as shown in the diagram, I might attempt to pot the brown because any good player would have little difficulty not only in negotiating the snooker from behind the green, but also doing so at exactly the strength to ensure that I would not have a pottable ball for my next shot. If I were to pot the brown, I would be four points better off and be in a

position to play a return-to-baulk safety shot. If I were to miss the pot, my opponent would have the chance of playing the return-to-baulk.

A decision whether to go for the brown would involve, of course, several factors, including the score, your opinion of your chances of potting the brown, your opinion of your opponent's safety play and so on. If you do not pot the brown, you will not leave your opponent in for a break but you may give him the chance to play a good return to the baulk cushion and, having split the reds open slightly with this shot, possibly leave you in a different position.

On most occasions therefore, I should still trickle up behind the green. My opponent would probably negotiate the snooker and not leave me a pottable red but, from behind the green, he would not be able to play a very positive shot.

Therefore, with my next shot I should again play to leave the cue-ball on the baulk cushion and at the same time possibly disturb the reds so that his next safety shot in reply will not be so easy for him. In other words, by trickling up behind the green I may not be able to force my opponent into an error immediately but, by keeping the upper hand tactically, I can give myself a good chance of doing so with my next shot or the shot after.

Things would be a little different if the cue-ball finishes in either Figure 78, Position 2 or Position 3. In Position 2, whether there were reds in the open or not, I would pot the brown and go up the table, either for a break or a safety-shot. The brown is after all a much easier pot from this position than from Position 1 nearly on the baulk cushion, and most players should be reasonably certain of potting it successfully. If there are some reds in the open, play to pot the brown and build up a break. If there is no possibility of getting on a red, then play for a good position from which to play a good safety shot.

If the cue-ball is in Position 3 the shot to play depends very much on the lie of the other balls. The brown is at the wrong angle to pot it and go up the table. Unless you can pot a red into the middle pocket or have a reasonably easy red into one of the top pockets, you might find that it would be wiser to trickle up behind the green, thus ensuring a probable good position for your next shot. However, should the reds be in a safe position accept four points for the brown which are yours for the taking and then play as good a safety shot as you can.

From my discussion of these positions have emerged two points which are often forgotten:

(1) Never refuse even a few easy points if you can help it; and

(2) Don't think that positional play is relevant only to break-building. It often pays to construct a break with the specific object, after a certain number of shots, of concluding it with a really good safety shot.

You might also bear in mind that the choice between attack and defence is often governed to a great extent by the state of the game and your opponent. There are, of course, certain positions from which you always play safe or always go for a break, no matter what the state of the game is or who your opponent is, but the good match player is one who can take in and act upon specific circumstances.

For instance, in a Youths' Snooker Championship Final (best of 5) some years ago, Cliff Wilson, potting them from everywhere, led me 2–0. Therefore, instead of continuing with my normal blend of attack and defence, I really closed the game up so that his form gradually began to deteriorate. As his confidence fell, mine rose, and I won 3–2.

However, in an Amateur Championship match I saw once, the opposite happened. One player had got it into his head that the way to win was to pot only balls which were near certainties and at the least suspicion of risk, play safe. Unfortunately for him, the other player's safety was quite good too and as he knocked in a few good long pots, the former soon found himself 2–0 down. Realizing that he was playing a bit too cautiously and not really giving his useful potting and break-building a chance he began to go for more and more, and soon drew up to 2–2.

Unfortunately, he again became too defence-minded and went down 3–2.

The lesson to be learnt here is that it is impossible to cut risk from the game entirely. To indulge in a lot of negative play (I do not mean constructive safety play) especially at the beginning of a game is really letting the other man get on top without his having to try to. The good tactician is not one who keeps rigidly to preconceived ideas but one who varies his game according to the situation.

There are certain positions one gets into at snooker when it is not practicable to build a break. Figure 79 is a case in point. I would like you to assume that there is a tight pack of six or seven reds between the pink and black spots and that there isn't a colour in a position to make it worth the risk of attempting to split the pack.

In a case like this some players would play off one of the baulk colours to leave the cue-ball on the baulk cushion. If you do this and leave your opponent a clear sight of the reds he may hit his safety shot a little too thick and give you a chance to make a break. On the other hand, there is a considerable risk that he will play a good safety shot and put you in trouble. If you leave your opponent snookered on the pack of reds he will roll up to them off a cushion, perhaps giving you four away, perhaps not.

I myself would not play a safety shot with a snooker off one of the baulk colours, although this would be better than the shot which can be seen in countless league games and friendlies. This shot, Shot 1, in Figure 79 consists of attempting to pot the blue **and** leave the cue-ball on the baulk cushion. If the pot is missed then there is no harm done. But if in fact the blue is potted you have got yourself into trouble which is very likely going to cost you a lot more than the five points you have earned from potting the blue.

Shot 2 in Figure 79 shows the shot I would play. I would still attempt to pot the blue but I would use stun to prevent the ball going any nearer baulk than I could help. Obviously, the nearer one is to a ball, either when playing a pot or safety shot, the better

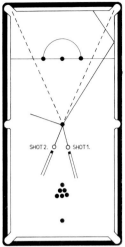

Fig. 79

39

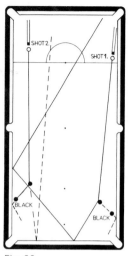

Fig. 80

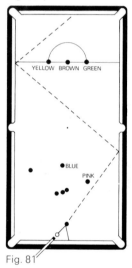

Fig. 81

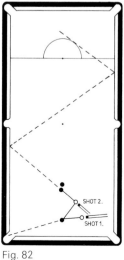

Fig. 82

chance there is of making exactly the contact one wants.

One of the things which tend to improve with experience is the ability to 'play the score'. Many inexperienced players think that, with the balls in a certain position, one should play the same shot, regardless of the score. Not so. In Figure 80, for instance, with one red left and the black in a safe position, you should play a different shot if you were 34 behind than you would if you were 34 in front.

There are two shots you can play if you need a red, a black and all the colours to win, both of them involving knocking the black into a more pottable position.

In Figure 80, Shot 1, you play to knock the red on to the black, as shown, and bring the cue-ball back to the baulk cushion. In Shot 2, which for simplicity I have drawn on the other side of the table, you play to double the red back to the baulk cushion and knock the black out with the cue-ball. Whichever shot you choose would depend on the precise position of the other balls. Less can go wrong with Shot 2 but, played well, Shot 1 can put your opponent in more trouble.

In Figure 81, we will assume that you are 58 in front with four reds left. Your opponent can win with four reds, four blacks and all the colours but not with four pinks. Therefore, the shot to play is one which will leave the black safe. As shown in my diagram, good judgement of weight will leave the black in the middle of the baulk cushion. It is also important to apply just the right amount of stun to leave the cue-ball tight on the top cushion so that your opponent does not have a chance to pot one of the reds in the middle pocket.

Figure 82 shows another case when it is better to ignore a potting opportunity in favour of a snooker. Once, having potted the last but one red, I needed two colours, the other red and all the colours and a snooker to win the frame.

My first idea was to pot the black, stun into position to pot the red into the opposite corner pocket, take another black and only then start thinking about how to get the snooker. On second thoughts, however, I potted the black and screwed back slightly so that, with my next shot, I could stun the red full in the face to send it into baulk as shown while leaving the cue-ball touching the pink. This left my opponent a really diabolical snooker and I won the frame. Had I not played this shot, it would have been extremely unlikely that, with all the colours on their spots, I could have laid anything near so effective a snooker.

When all the colours are on their spots, it is a good position for clearing the table but a very unpromising one for laying snookers because all the balls are in the open. The chances of laying a snooker are much greater when you have a colour or two not on but slightly away from a cushion.

Figure 83 shows the position left after your opponent had failed to hit one of your snookers. He has left a free ball with a chance of taking the brown into the middle pocket and going up the table for the black.

I would decide against this because I feel that there is a strong possibility of missing the brown. I would probably not leave my opponent in a position to pot the red but he would have been well placed to put me in a lot of trouble with an agressive safety shot. Therefore, put the onus on him by making him play again, knowing that the middle pocket was interfering with the natural side cushion angle to hit the red.

Figure 84 on the other hand, shows a position where I would attempt to get in for a break rather than play what would have to be a fairly negative safety shot. There is a red in a nicely pottable position in the baulk area which rules out any idea of leaving the cue-ball in that part of the table. There is also a red a little way from the side cushion and 30 centimetres (a foot) or so from the middle pocket.

The shot to play here is a cross double into the opposite middle pocket, bringing the cue-ball back towards the top cushion. You may bring the cue-ball back dead to the top cushion or you may leave it slightly away from it, a position from which you could, if necessary, pot the black. Either way, you cannot go far

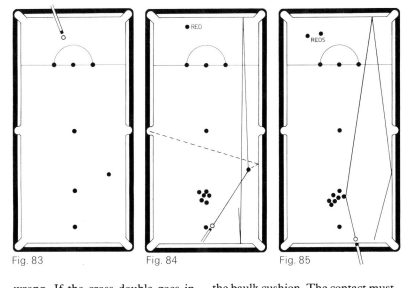

Fig. 83   Fig. 84   Fig. 85   Fig. 86

wrong. If the cross double goes in, you may have a chance to get in with a break: if it doesn't, you should leave the balls safe for your opponent.

Figure 85 shows another position in which it is necessary to bring the cue-ball back to the top cushion because there are a couple of pottable reds in the baulk area. Play thinly off the pack of reds and try to make sure, before you play your shot, that the pack is not arranged in such a way that you are likely to knock a red near a pocket for your opponent.

In Figure 86, the angle of the cue-ball to the pack is such that you cannot get the cue-ball back to the top cushion. Neither can you leave the cue-ball in the baulk area because of those two pottable reds. The shot to play here is a thin snick off the outer red of the pack to leave the cue-ball dead on the side cushion with the green stopping your opponent having a go at either of the two reds in baulk. In fact, the only reply your opponent can make is a slow roll to the pack, a negative shot from which you may be able to play a really aggressive safety shot at your next visit.

Shot 1 in Figure 87 shows a position in which many players do not realize that a safety shot is 'on'. Even though the object-ball may be only a centimetre (half-an-inch) from the side cushion it is still possible by hitting it very thinly to get the cue-ball back up the table, as shown, while leaving the object-ball safe near

the baulk cushion. The contact must, of course, be very thin as the cue-ball must have gone beyond the point that the continuous and dotted lines cross before the object-ball does so – otherwise the balls will kiss and an easy position be left for your opponent.

Figure 87, Shot 2 – a similar shot but allowing more margin of error than Shot 1 – is one of my favourites. It is a shot that cannot go far wrong but if one gauges one's weight just right one can leave the object-ball on or very near the baulk cushion and the cue-ball similarly placed at the other end of the table – in the kind of position I hope my opponent will never leave me.

In Figure 87, Shot 1, most players would be happy to avoid leaving their opponent with an easy chance. However, one of the things which distinguishes the 'class' player from the 'good' player is the ability, when left in a difficult position, to leave his opponent in a position which is even worse. In this position, therefore, the 'class' player or the player who aspires to become one, will not play to leave the object-ball safe but will attempt to leave the cue-ball on the top cushion, as shown.

Figure 88 is a typical billiards player's shot in that it is reminiscent of many a two cushion cannon with which a player hopes to keep a break going in an unpromising position. I should emphasize that in this shot the object-ball is returned to the baulk

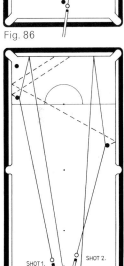

Fig. 87

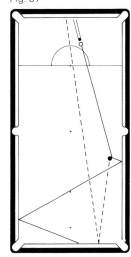

Fig. 88

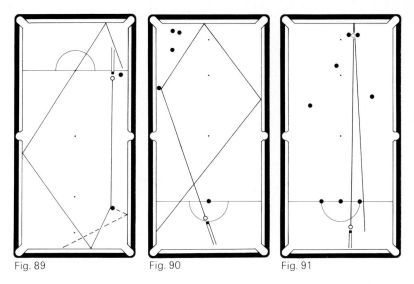

Fig. 89 Fig. 90 Fig. 91

cushion while the cue-ball travels off two cushions to finish on the top cushion.

The shot shown in Figure 89 is also of the type at which billiards players seem to excel. The object-ball in this case is the pink and I am assuming that the striker needs a snooker and both remaining balls to win. This type of shot looks simple on a diagram but a lot of practice and experience are needed.

Billiards, of course, gives the knowledge of angles which is so necessary to execute a shot like this. It is not so generally realized that billiards gives a wonderful training for assessing 'weight'. After all, it is not much use getting the cue-ball travelling on the right path to get it behind the black if you play the shot half a metre (a foot or two) too slow or too hard.

Finally, for this chapter, a couple of somewhat unusual but nevertheless useful ways of 'getting back down'. With neither shot can one gauge the exact final position of the cue-ball accurately but one can gauge it well enough to ensure that immediate danger is avoided.

In Figure 90 there is no chance of a pot and, at a first glance, not much chance of leaving one's opponent safe either. The correct shot to play is a ricochet off the red lying tight on the side cushion. Address the cue-ball low and play with more than medium strength, hard enough to bring the

cue-ball back to the position shown. In the case of a ricochet, striking the cue-ball with top produces a smothering effect on contact with the object-ball and reduces the run of the cue-ball afterwards. A double kiss often occurs and so much backspin is produced that it is almost impossible to get the cue-ball back down the table. Therefore, when playing this kind of ricochet, strike the cue-ball low. It will increase the run of the cue-ball.

In Figure 91, the striker again had no chance of a pot and no chance of an orthodox safety shot. Because of the reds lying near the middle pocket it is imperative to bring the cue-ball back into the baulk area.

It is a good general rule to beware of safety shots which involve contact with more than one ball, but Figure 91 is one of the few exceptions to this. It is possible to contact two reds almost simultaneously at roughly the same thickness. One can, therefore, predict with some certainty that the cue-ball will return towards baulk to a safe position as shown.

Chapter Eight
Snookering

A good general rule for snookering and safety play is: if laying a snooker, try to open the balls up; if getting out of a snooker, avoid opening them up.

In Figure 92, Shot 1, many players would be content to play thinly off the end red, hardly disturbing the pack and leave the cue-ball on the baulk cushion. Agreed that the cue-ball should be left on the baulk cushion, but one's opponent will be in far more difficulty if the pack of reds is opened. Therefore, the correct shot is to play a thicker contact on the end-red – even using some screw if necessary, and take the cue-ball down the table as I have shown in the diagram.

Shot 1 in Figure 93 shows another snooker which can be made more aggressive if the pack is split. A safety shot could be played by using right-hand side and taking the cue-ball between the blue and the opposite middle pocket. The correct shot, however, is to take the cue-ball the baulk side of the blue with a slight screw to get behind the yellow and brown, 'pot' the red on to the pack, thus opening most of them into a pottable position.

Similarly with Shot 2 in Figure 93, my advice is consciously to make a point of doubling the red which is near the cushion into the pack of reds. If you do not open the reds with shots like this you will find that, even if you have laid a snooker, your opponent will trickle up to the reds. He may, of course, not judge the angle from the cushion correctly but even so this will only add four to your score. With the reds open it will probably be impossible for him to trickle up to a ball and the chances are that you will be able to get in with a useful break.

Shot 1, in Figure 94, is yet another shot when most players hit the red very thin to get down the table. In this position I would make about a half ball contact and use strong right-hand side so that the cue-ball would still get behind the baulk colours.

In Shot 2 in Figure 94 most players would play thinly off the red nearest baulk. This might leave one red in a pottable position but would still leave the other two reds, which are touching, not pottable. I would therefore play off the red nearest the top cushion and let the cue-ball flick off the second red, as shown to go down to the baulk cushion. All three reds would thus be in pottable positions.

Two further comments about this shot. First, you need a good knowledge of billiards to be certain that the cue-ball will in fact contact the middle red thinly enough to get to the baulk cushion. If in fact it contacts it thickly, the cue-ball will remain in the top half of the table to give your opponent an easy opening. Second (and this applies to a lesser degree in all the shots I have discussed), you have to be careful that you don't send any of the reds too near a pocket. Opening a pack of reds is one thing, leaving one or more reds right over the pocket is another. In the second case if the cue-ball does not go right behind a colour you have presented your opponent with an easy opening. Therefore, before you play any of the shots I have described, study reds to avoid, as far as you can, leaving a red over a pocket.

Shot 2 in Figure 92 belongs to a different type. This position occurred in the deciding stage of an Amateur Championship match. The player in play needed only one ball to win. The ball 'on' was the green. Quite correctly, he tried to pot it in the top pocket but he made the mistake of trying to get position on the brown. If he had played the shot as I've shown in my diagram, leaving the cue-ball right behind the brown it wouldn't have mattered if he'd missed the green. As it was, however, he not only missed the green but gave his opponent a chance to pot it and take the remaining colours for the match. Had the striker needed two balls to win instead of one the shot he

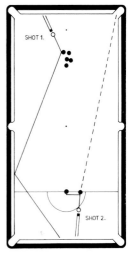

Fig. 92

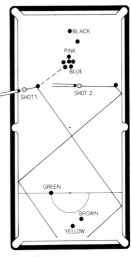

Fig. 93

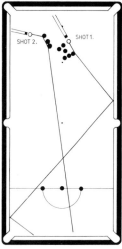

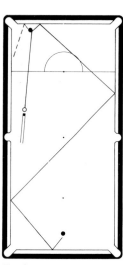

Fig. 94

played would have been the right one. I am not sure whether he played the wrong shot because he didn't realize he needed only one ball to win or because the tension affected his judgement. Either way, it was a mistake that could have been avoided with an extra moment's consideration.

It is comparatively rare in a frame played by two players of more or less equal ability to find a player who needs a snooker on the last two or three balls going on to win the frame. Over an extended period I don't suppose the proportion of frames won from this position is more than one or possibly two out of ten. Yet I remember going for months without winning a frame from this position and then winning two in a row. Needing a snooker on the last two or three balls is a situation in which no one can regard himself as favourite to win the frame, but, even if one doesn't win the frame, one can sometimes give one's opponent a few anxious moments. If one does upset the odds and win a frame from this losing position it gives you a great psychological lift and leaves your opponent demoralized and kicking himself for losing a frame he should have won.

It has become a truism that a knowledge of billiards is invaluable for good snookering and safety-play. Figure 95 is an example. If a player knows the route the cue-ball ought to take to get the all-round cannon, then he also knows the route to get the cue-ball behind the black for a snooker. One point to remember about this shot is to be sure to leave the object-ball in the baulk half of the table – not bring it into the top half as you would do for positional reasons if you play the cannon at billiards. Of course, the pink and black are so far apart that no one on earth can guarantee a snooker from this position. However, a few minutes practice on this shot will give you some guidance on assessing angles, whether you need to use side, and so on, which will improve your chances of getting a snooker behind the black when a similar position turns up in a match.

Another position which often crops up when you are trying to lay

Fig. 95

snookers is shown in Figure 96. Here again, success depends on a good knowledge of angles and good control of weight – another quality which billiards tends to develop very well.

Sometimes, in this kind of position, a snooker is made that much more awkward by the middle pocket being 'in the way'. By this, I mean that the natural angle for getting out of the snooker involved hitting a cushion just where the middle pocket is. To avoid the middle pocket, side has to be used and this, of course, makes the shot more difficult, especially on tables you don't know very well.

Often, the middle pocket gets in the way through no particular thought by the player laying the snooker but it is sometimes possible to do this by intention. To perform this, one has to visualize, in planning the snooker, at what angle one's opponent will need to hit the cushion to get out of it and adjust one's shot accordingly.

One mistake I see players making wherever I go is illustrated by Figure 97. Many players, if they are 20 behind on the blue, appear to think that it is automatically in their interests to keep the blue on the table. They are working on the assumption that the more balls there are, the more chance there is of getting a snooker. There are many cases, however, when the blue should be potted and the position in Figure 97 is one of them.

When doing so, however, one should play the pot with a view to getting in the best possible position to lay a snooker. Many players appear to think that one can lay a snooker from almost anywhere but, in fact, getting the cue-ball in a good position is half the battle.

Another point about potting balls when one still needs snookers is this: suppose you are 28 in front on the yellow and your opponent refuses pots and tries for snookers. Don't you feel comforted by the fact that even if he does eventually lay a snooker (and you miss it) he has still got to pot six balls? On the other hand, if he takes yellow, green and brown and you see that he is about to lay a nasty snooker on the blue, you will probably begin

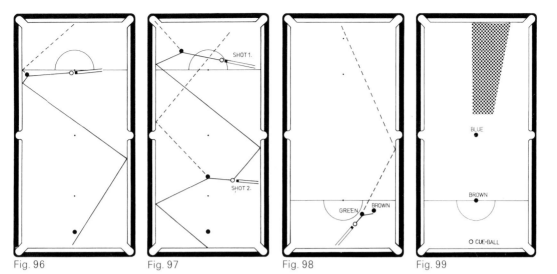

Fig. 96   Fig. 97   Fig. 98   Fig. 99

to sweat for a bit, for, if you fail to get out of the snooker, he has to pot only three balls to win. Therefore potting some balls and then snookering 'at the death' puts more pressure on the player in front.

Finally, how often have I seen a player struggling like mad to get a snooker or even two snookers and then, needing only two or three balls to win, fail to get them? This is sometimes because a player may have put so much mental effort and energy into getting the snookers that he then lets his concentration slip a little.

On the other hand, concentration is often the factor which separates the very good players from the good. A good player might have the technique to get the snookers but might then miss an easy one through unconsciously relaxing his concentration: a very good player realizes that getting snookers is no use without potting the balls as well – and keeps his concentration 'switched on' accordingly.

When playing a snooker, don't put the object-ball over a pocket. If you're not sure of getting the snooker, you leave your opponent 'in' almost for certain: even if you are sure of laying a snooker, don't leave the object-ball hanging over a pocket because your opponent, if he negotiates the snooker, will probably pot the object-ball as well. Second, if you're sure of getting a snooker try to keep the object-ball away from a cushion and thus prevent your oppo-

nent from rolling up to it at dead weight. Figure 98 shows what I mean. Many players would simply roll the green past the brown but I would prefer to put more distance between the ball by stunning behind the brown as I have shown.

Figure 99 shows how conveniently placed the brown and blue spots are when you are trying to lay a snooker with the cue-ball in baulk and the object-ball in an area between the pink and black spots. If the brown and blue are both on their spots it is surprising what a large area of the table they obscure. My diagram shows the cue-ball on the baulk cushion and I have shaded out the area of the table in which it would be impossible to get through direct to an object-ball.

Figure 100 shows the same kind of thing happening with the green and blue and yellow and blue. A thorough knowledge of the ways and means of getting the cue-ball on the baulk cushion and the object-ball somewhere in the appropriate shaded area, is one of the main factors in successful snookering.

Figure 101, Shot 1, shows a position where even a novice would find it easy to lay a snooker. All he has to do is to play the last red slowly up the table (having contacted it just over half-ball) and roll up behind the yellow. However, this is not the best way to play the shot because, unless the cue-ball finishes either touching

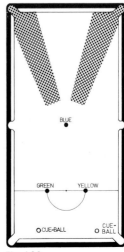

Fig. 100

45

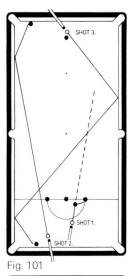

Fig. 101

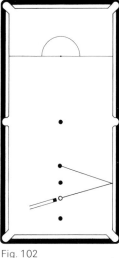

Fig. 102

Fig. 103

or practically touching the yellow, the next player would have a quite simple 'escape route' via the side cushion. The snooker would be much more aggressive if a soft stun stroke was used to send the red further up the table, still taking great care, of course, to tuck the cue-ball as closely behind the yellow as you can.

This method of playing the snooker is much better than the novice's method because it not only makes the red more difficult to hit but increases the chances that you will have a good opening next shot. One last word on this position, though; be careful not to send the red under a cushion. It is true that your opponent may still be unable to hit the red, but, even if he doesn't, the chances are you will not have an easy leave. The gaining of penalty points from snooker is usually secondary in importance to forcing your opponent to give you an easy opening.

In Figure 101, Shot 2, for instance you must think beyond just hitting the red and avoiding giving four away. Play this shot very slowly so that the cue-ball just reaches the red **on the pocket side.** If you were to contact the right-hand side of the red (looking from baulk) then you would almost certainly present your opponent with a gift opening, probably to clear the table. It is far better to err on the side of safety even if it means missing the red altogether on the pocket side. It is better to give four away than an almost certain eight or more. I am not, of course, advocating a deliberate miss.

Try to hit the red but make sure that you do so (a) on the pocket side, as shown in the diagram, and (b) at dead weight, to eliminate the possibility of pushing the red into a pottable position.

The same applies in Figure 101, Shot 3. Don't be afraid to use more than one cushion (even if you can get out of the snooker by using one only) if you can thereby reduce the risk of leaving your opponent a good position. In Figure 101, Shot 3, even if the baulk colours were not in the way, it would be better to use two cushions instead of one. In this way you can again ensure that the cue-ball either contacts the red on the pocket side or

else just misses it on that side, in either case leaving it safe.

It is necessary to know the strength at which to play shots. Whereas Shots 2 and 3 in Figure 101 have to be played at dead weight, that is, at just sufficient strength to reach the object-ball, the shot in Figure 102 should be played briskly.

If the shot is played slowly, you are 95 per cent certain, whether you hit the red or not, of leaving your opponent with an easy position. However, if you play the shot briskly you have a good chance of either knocking the red to a reasonably safe position or making the cue-ball skim past the red at enough speed to ensure that, if your opponent has a possible pot, it is not a certainty. In other words, if there is a risk of leaving the ball on, play the shot hard so that there is more chance of putting distance between the cue-ball and object-ball when they come to rest.

Of course, there is an element of luck in all this but forcing you to rely partially on luck is all to the credit of the man who laid the snooker. This illustrates in another way the point I made in Figure 101, Shot 1, about it being more difficult both to negotiate a snooker and leave your opponent safe when the object-ball is in the open. In Figure 102, a good player should be reasonably certain of hitting the red but as for leaving his opponent in a safe position, he can only 'hit and hope'.

By playing the shot briskly, he can reduce the chance of leaving his opponent in, but he cannot eliminate the chance altogether.

The difficult part of some shots is recognizing that they are on.

Figure 103 shows a position in which it is quite easy to lay a snooker but it is a shot which does not occur to everyone. The correct shot is to hit the red about half ball, just hard enough for it to reach beyond the middle pocket, as shown. The cue-ball will then cannon off the blue and go behind the brown and yellow. One of the beauties of this shot is that the cue ball's contact on the blue, the second object-ball, can be almost anything from quarter-ball to three-quarter ball for you still to be virtually certain of laying a snooker.

Chapter Nine
All on the Black

I have heard many players say 'I was unlucky. I lost 3–2. I beat him out of sight two frames and he won three on the black.'

What these players often mean is that they missed a chance to consolidate an early lead or, more often, that they did not play as well in the close frames as they did when they were miles in front.

The closer the frame, the more important it is to keep cool. Don't refuse reasonable chances but don't seize them too hastily. Try to maintain your usual rhythm. Don't play faster in your anxiety to get the frame won; don't play slower trying to make extra sure. Try to approach the shot on its merits; don't let thoughts of what that shot means in terms of winning a frame impinge on your concentration. I know that some of these things are very difficult to do but close matches are usually won by those whose mental self-discipline is greatest in a crisis.

Figures 104 and 105 show two end-of-frame positions which all require a cool head.

In Figure 104, the cue-ball has come into such a position on the pink that it is not hard to pot the pink but not easy to get on the black. Most players, if they are attempting to get on the black, try to pot the pink very slowly so that the cue-ball does not bounce too far off the cushion and out of position for the black. I don't recommend this method because you may be so pre-occupied with holding your position on the black that you don't hit the pink hard enough and leave it near the middle pocket for your opponent.

Alternatively, you may make sure of the pink but come too far for the black. So why not play considerably harder and come round for the black off three cushions instead of one? Some people, I know, do not like potting at anything more speedy than a crawl into the middle pockets, but this is a fear that they have somehow

to put behind them. If the ball is hit properly then, at any reasonable speed, it will go in. Even if it doesn't in this particular case, the pink should come far enough away from the pocket to prevent your opponent from having an easy shot.

Figure 105, Shot 1, is always apt to come up. The object-ball may not always be the black, as in this case, but nevertheless, it is a shot which, when mastered, can come in useful at all sorts of times. The black is about eight centimetres (three inches) from the top pocket and about the same from the side cushion. The cue-ball is on the baulk cushion, dead straight on the black. As the cushion prevents you from getting under the cue-ball to apply enough back spin to stop it following the object-ball into the pocket, the only way to pot the black and avoid the in-off is to strike the cushion a little distance from the black.

With this shot you must have the courage to hit the cushion far enough away from the black. The most common fault, probably stemming from a fear of missing the object-ball altogether, is to hit the cushion too near the object-ball. However, there is really nothing to the shot once you have it firmly in your mind what to do. On the other hand, don't be too keen to use this shot if the object-ball is very much farther away from the cushion than it is in this case, as I have found by experience that such shots are extremely chancey.

What is the best thing to do when a frame finishes in a tie – meaning of course that the black has to be re-spotted? This situation sometimes occurs in matches and it is not a bad idea to have a shot worked out for such an emergency.

First of all, the best possible action is to win the toss which decides who has first shot at the black. If I win the toss on these occasions I always put my opponent into bat, knowing full well that no matter what he plays or

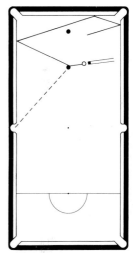

Fig. 104

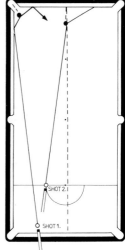

Fig. 105

who he is there is at least a fifty-fifty chance of the shot going wrong.

However, we will assume that you have lost the toss and have to play the first shot. I would advise you to spot as near the green as possible and, going across the black slightly, attempt by means of a three-quarter ball contact to bring the black back as near to the middle of the baulk cushion as possible as I have shown in Figure 105, Shot 2.

On a really first class table I would actually place the cue-ball on the green spot but on most club tables there is a chance of the cue-ball jumping a little if it has been placed on a spot – not much maybe but enough to matter.

The shot can go wrong in several ways. You can get slightly too full a contact on the black and thus get a kiss which would probably leave an easy black for your opponent in a top pocket; you can catch the black slightly too thin and thus double it over the baulk pocket; or you can catch the black much too thin and leave it over the middle pocket. Even if your contact is perfect, a slight imperfection in the weight of the shot can let you down. Hit the black too hard or too slow and you leave your opponent a chance of potting it in the baulk pocket.

You must think that with all these things liable to go wrong with the shot that there must be an easier one. Believe me, there isn't. Some players like to play from the green spot to snick the black under the side cushion and return round the table towards and beyond the green shot. With this shot, however, you risk hitting the cue-ball hard enough to return to the baulk cushion when there is a distinct chance of going in-off in the baulk pocket. At the best, with this alternative shot, you are bound to leave your opponent either a possible pot or a fairly easy safety shot. However, with the shot I recommend, there is a good chance, if you play it well, of putting your opponent in real trouble. As regards possible shots to play in this situation it is by far the best of an unpleasant bunch.

The author, Rex Williams, in play in a competition.

Chapter Ten
Plants and Sets

First of all, let me define what is meant by the terms 'plant' and 'set'. A set is when two balls are touching in such a way that a fullish contact on the first ball, for example ball 'A', in Figure 106, Shot 1, will pot the second ball, ball 'B'.

A plant is a position where the two balls are not touching, for example balls 'X' and 'Y' in Figure 107, Shot 1, but in which, by knocking the first ball, 'X', on to the second ball, 'Y', at a particular angle the second ball may be potted.

So far, this is elementary but already I may have raised one point which the reader may find strange. In my second sentence, I specifically mentioned 'a fullish contact' as being necessary to pot the second ball even when the balls are set.

'But surely,' you ask, 'it doesn't matter what angle you hit the first ball at. If the two balls are touching then surely the second ball must be potted.' This sounds logical enough, I agree, but let us try a simple trest.

As shown in Figure 106, Shot 1, place two balls, 'A' and 'B', for a set. From the position shown, hit red 'A' full in the face. Naturally, you will pot red 'B'. Then replace the balls in the same position but this time hit red 'A' about quarter ball so that the cue-ball travels towards the top cushion. You will also find, rather surprisingly, that red 'B' will hit a point a short way up the side cushion.

Joe Davis used to explain that this is due to a squeeze taking place between the three balls at the moment of impact. However, with all due respect to Joe, I do not think that squeeze is the right term. If a squeeze actually takes place then surely the second object-ball should hit the top not the side cushion.

Let us now carry our experiment a little further. Once more, replace balls 'A' and 'B' in the same position but, before you do so, wet those parts of the two balls which touch each other. Once again, hit ball 'A' about

quarter ball exactly as you did before. This time, ball 'B' will be potted.

How is it that ball 'B' is potted when its point of contact is wet but not when it is dry? Here is my theory.

When the balls are dry, I believe there is an indiscernible 'tackiness' attached to them which causes, in the case of a set, the second object-ball to stay with the first object-ball for a fraction of a second. Perhaps I should explain this rather more fully. Imagine that only ball 'A' is in this diagram and that you are hitting it quarter-ball as before. Ball 'A' will of course hit well up the side cushion. Even when ball 'B' is resting against it, ball 'A' is still, as it were, when hit in this way, struggling to hit that same spot on the side cushion and that slight tackiness, as I mentioned, causes ball 'A' to take ball 'B' a short way off its angled journey until the forward force generated by the impact of the cue-ball reasserts itself and ball 'B' 'remembers', as it were, that it is meant to be going into the pocket and straightens up, though not of course sufficently. Incidentally, this effect occurs even when balls 'A' and 'B' are anything from touching to three millimetres (an eighth of an inch) apart and the use of side makes no difference to this particular shot.

What are the practical applications of this? First, I hope I have disproved the old fallacy that the second object-ball of a set must be potted regardless of how the first object-ball is hit. Second, with your new knowledge, you will begin to realize that certain balls are set (and thus pottable) which you previously thought were not set (and thus not pottable). I have given an example of what I mean in Figure 106, Shot 2. Strike the first object-ball on the left and the second object-ball will be potted.

Now, however, a word about plants. These, of course, are much harder than sets in that one ball has to be precisely 'potted' on to another

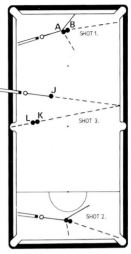

Fig. 106

ball so that the latter enters the pocket. Look now at Figure 107, Shot 1. Clearly, the only way in which a ball can be potted in this position is to knock ball 'X' on to ball 'Y'. This is my procedure in a case like this.

I first address ball 'X' as if I am going to use it as the cue-ball with which to pot ball 'Y'. I thus know what place on ball 'Y' ball 'X' has to contact. However, as a further check, I aim to 'pot' ball 'X' on to a point 'P' a few inches up the side cushion. It is essential that ball 'X' travels along a direct line towards point 'P' if ball 'Y' is to be potted.

To some readers, this may seem needlessly complicated. 'Why not simply aim for a particular spot on the second object-ball?' they may ask. This opinion may be partly though not entirely justified with a shot such as Figure 107, Shot 1 because the pot is a fairly straight one. However, when the plant has to be made on more of an angle, then the point 'P', as I have shown it in Figure 107, Shot 2 is indispensable.

The ability to detect plants can be very useful for 'shots to nothing' – attempting a plant and at the same time playing a safety return to the baulk cushion. Imagine, for instance, that you are playing a safety shot off ball 'E' in Figure 107, Shot 3. If ball 'E' is hit in a certain way then ball 'F' can be potted.

You should try to sort out these plants, not only in attempting to pot balls, but as an insurance against potting balls you don't want to pot. For instance, if ball 'F' is the pink and ball 'E' is a red then you must obviously use your knowledge to avoid a plant. One word of warning: do not allow yourself to become too fond of playing shots to nothing consisting of a possible plant and a return to baulk. All too often in doing this, a player falls between two stools: he misses the plant, leaves a pottable ball near a pocket and fails to return at all near the baulk cushion. As a general rule for playing this type of shot, try first and foremost to play a good safety shot. If you can achieve this, nothing can go wrong.

That well-known film, *The*

Hustler, has as its background the American game of Pool. In fact, a good deal of the film is taken up with two matches between Minnesota Fats and Fast Eddie, purportedly the two best players in America and the scenes showing the matches between these two are extremely well done with Willie Mosconi (on the credit titles as technical adviser) actually playing many of the shots we see. Some of them may seem rather far fetched to us but we must remember that the pockets on the American table are approx. 12½ centimetres (five inches) wide compared with our nine centimetres (three and a half inches). Admittedly, the balls are slightly larger and heavier but nevertheless, by any standards, Pool pockets must be considered pretty easy.

If you bear this in mind it is not surprising that plants and sets play such an important part in Pool. I remember when George Chenier of Canada came to Britain he showed everybody a thing or three about plants and sets. He used to spend long periods studying the lie of as many as a dozen balls before producing some fantastic shot or other. In fact, the British professionals were soon to be seen carrying out the same procedure, though none of them ever attained George's standard at this kind of thing. I remember in particular one shot he played, not because it was very difficult but because of the way he got down and played the shot as a matter of course almost without thinking. This shot is Shot 3 in Figure 106.

There were three reds 'J', 'K' and 'L' in the middle of the table. 'K' and 'L' touching, blocked the path to the pocket of 'J'. Fortunately, 'K' and 'L' were set for a pot in the middle pocket though the cue-ball, of course, was on the wrong side of the table to hit them. George solved this problem by doubling red 'J' so that it cannoned into red 'K', thus potting red 'L'.

This sort of shot is commonplace in Pool and I think that if a British player had a chance to play this game a great deal his standard at plants and sets in Snooker would automatically rise.

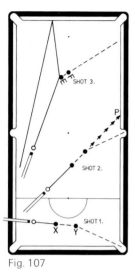

Fig. 107

Chapter Eleven
The Nap

It is an amazing thing that people can play billiards and snooker for thirty or forty years without realizing that the application of side to the cue-ball will have an entirely opposite effect to the normal one of playing up the table (away from baulk) if the shot is played down the table (towards baulk).

Billiards and snooker are not played on wood or formica or glass but on a baize cloth. If you run your hand along the cloth towards the top cushion you will notice that it feels far smoother than if you do so towards baulk. This, of course, is because of the nap of the cloth.

We will suppose for the moment that you are using right-hand side with the nap, that's away from baulk. The initial blow which is struck at the right-hand side of the ball will send it out to the left. But the spin quickly corrects this and soon the cue-ball begins to spin to the right. If, however, you were playing with right-hand side towards baulk, that is against the nap, the cue-ball will not recover from the initial push-out to the left. On the contrary, as long as the side is still operating it will curl farther and farther to the left.

In connection with this, here is a tip for billiards players. If you are playing towards baulk and you have a rather narrow in-off for which you think you need check side, either choose another shot or try to get the in-off by a thinner but plain-ball contact. If you do use check side, it is most unlikely that the cue-ball will go anywhere near the pocket.

Conversely, it is occasionally possible, though I would recommend it only as a last resort, to get an otherwise impossible in-off by cramming on as much check side as possible; in fact exactly the reverse of the side you would normally expect and would use if you were playing with instead of against the nap.

Figure 108, Shot 1, is a shot which I employ quite often. There is one red

left and you need that, a colour, and all the colours to win. The angle is wrong to run through on the black and any plain ball pot will involve kissing the pink. Even if the latter were not so, one ought to bear in mind that the pink is not the easiest of balls with which to gain position on the small colours.

The correct shot to play in this case is to pot with screw and left-hand side. You will find that the cue-ball will first spring off at a sharp enough angle to miss the pink. It will at first seem that the cue-ball is going to finish close to the blue but soon the combined effect of side and nap will come into play and the cue-ball will curve gently away from the blue. If you have judged the weight of the stroke correctly, you should be ideally placed for potting the blue and obtaining perfect position to clear the colours.

Figure 108, Shot 2 shows how you can again make use of the nap of the cloth. The object of this shot is to pot the black and obtain position on the yellow. The black should be potted with a combination of screw and right-hand side. On contacting the black the cue-ball will spring away at an angle which, if it continued on the same course would take the ball between the green and its corner baulk pocket.

However, at approximately the time the cue-ball passes the pink the side begins to take effect and straighten the cue-ball up. If the weight is judged correctly an excellent position on the yellow should result. In my opinion, this is a particularly useful shot because it overcomes two obstacles at once. It eliminates a possibility of kissing the pink and also prevents the cue-ball from finishing near enough to the side cushion to make the following pot of the yellow awkward.

It is a good idea to practise the shots mentioned here, to get to know the effect of the nap.

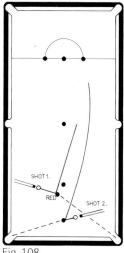

Fig. 108

Chapter Twelve
Adjusting to Different Conditions

It is amazing with a game like snooker, always played indoors, with the same sized balls, on the same size tables, and so on, that one can get so much variation in the conditions under which one plays. In fact, the longer I play the more I'm convinced that one never gets two sets of playing conditions the same.

Two identically-made tables may leave the works at exactly the same time and yet when the tables come to be erected they will have small but nevertheless noticeable differences. One of the things which only experience can give is the ability to adjust oneself to different tables. The professional playing in a different club almost every night of the week has every chance to acquire it if he is to play well enough to keep getting engagements.

I must admit, though, that there are some tables which make it impossible for a player to produce anywhere near his true form. The worst thing that can happen is that the pockets can be so tight that it is impossible to pot a ball down a cushion or at speed when one has less than the full face of the pocket to aim at.

Many clubs know that their tables have unduly tight pockets but don't do anything about it on the grounds that 'when they get on easier tables, the pockets look like buckets'. There is a certain amount of truth in this but it is also true that playing too much on a table which is too tight leads to a defensive approach to the game. Knowing how difficult it is to make a break, players tend to be content with taking a red and a colour and playing safe – an approach they find difficult to shake off when they get on a table on which break-making is possible.

Tight pockets are only one of the things which can affect your play, of course, but they stand out as the only thing you can't do anything about

when you are playing. Many tables run off, for instance, but you can minimize the effect of this aspect of imperfect playing conditions by not playing any ball slowly when there is any other possible way of playing the shot.

Thus, on tables I can't trust to run true, I find myself playing certain shots as a stun run through, which on a perfect table I would be content to play slowly and let the cue-ball run through of its own accord. Slow shots played either against or across the nap tend to be especially treacherous so wherever possible I play them with enough speed to make sure that (a) the cue-ball does not run off before it gets to the object-ball and (b) that the object-ball will not run off while it is on its way to the pocket.

Two variable facts which a player has to consider every time he plays are speed of the table and the state of the nap. I must add a third factor – quality of the cloth. The coarser the cloth, the more likely one is to slip up when using side.

A situation in which two reds near the top cushion prevent you getting position by stunning off the top cushion, shows how the first two factors can determine one's choice of shot. On a slow table with a heavy nap, the correct shot would be to pot the red with a slow screw to hold the cue-ball in position for the black. On a fast table on which the nap has worn thin this might be either impossible or not worth risking. The shot to play in this case would be a screw with right-hand side to swing the cue-ball off two cushions. The cue-ball is struck with right-hand side and rather less screw for this shot.

There are, of course, many intermediate stages between 'slow tables with heavy nap' and 'fast tables with very little nap'. In each case you have to choose your shot according to the conditions. Experienced players invariably take all these factors into account unconsciously when selecting their shot. It is well to remember also that two or three centimetres (an inch) either way can often decide whether a soft screw is on as a means of getting position.

What other factors can affect your normal game? Are all windows completely blacked out? If there is too much light in places other than over the table, the limits of the table, particularly the pockets, become less well defined and the spectators and other distractions become all that easier to see.

Is the cloth brand new and shiny? Shots with side are easily missed on any table with a new cloth, especially if it has a noticeable sheen on it through ironing. When one uses, say, right-hand side on this type of cloth, the cue-ball pushes out initially much farther to the left before swinging to the right. Thus a shot one normally doesn't think twice about, like a black off its spot with a touch of side, becomes fraught with danger.

A freshly covered table is wonderful to play on once one is used to it but not so easy if one is used to playing on cloths which are thinner or coarser.

On my travels round the clubs I play on quite a few tables which have been re-covered especially for my exhibition. This brings me up against the problem of the 'sliding' cushion and I often have to adjust my game to deal with it, since the balls tend to take a wider angle off the cushion.

Alex Higgins, World Professional Snooker Champion, 1972 and 1982.

53

Chapter Thirteen
The Mental Approach

When summer comes I, like many snooker professionals, like to get out on a golf course and, as a change from trying to make centuries, try to avoid making them – that is, get round in less than a hundred strokes. To me, golf is a fascinating game, and it occurred to me some time ago, when reading an article of Henry Longhurst's in the *Sunday Times*, how similar it was in some respects to billiards and snooker. These similarities do not occur much in the technique of the two sports – you'd look a bit silly trying to pot a ball with the inter-locking grip – but certain mental attitudes practised by leading golfers hold good for aspiring snooker players.

One of Mr Longhurst's chief points in the article was that the rise of Japan in golfing circles was attributable to their native imperturbability 'which gives them a wonderful eye and hand and no nerves.' Believe me, a snooker player needs these qualities just as much as a golfer. For instance, how steady is your bridge hand when the cue-ball is tight under the cushion and you have to elevate your cue much more than usual to strike the ball? How steady is your bridge hand normally? Is it perfectly still or, in a tight match, does it tend to waver slightly? If it does waver, really grip the cloth with your bridge hand. I grip the cloth so hard sometimes that my fingers go chalk white. Do you sometimes miscue when you use side? If you do, I suppose you put it down to either a bad tip, not enough chalk or striking too much on the side of the ball. Any of these things could be responsible for a miscue but you could unthinkingly be dipping your bridge hand as you swing the cue in an unconscious effort to get a more vicious spin on the cue-ball.

This often arises through a player addressing the cue-ball centrally at first and then deciding that the shot he is about to play needs some side. Instead of moving his feet and his

bridge hand, he merely points his tip obliquely at the edge of the ball so that he is, in fact, hitting across the ball instead of through it. This, of course, makes a proper follow-through impossible and in an attempt to finish the shot with the cue following through in a straight line, the bridge hand is dipped.

Mr Longhurst notes approvingly in his article that the Japanese are on the whole quick and decisive players, and here again billiards and snooker players can learn from this. 'When one's mind is made up,' says Mr Longhurst, 'there is only a short period of mental concentration left in which to actually make the effort.' In general, the quicker you are making up your mind about a shot, the more mentally alert you tend to be.

It is painful sometimes to see good players, poised in indecision, taking an eternity to select the shot they are going to play. Funnily enough, the longer they take, the likelier they are to make a mess of it. The more possibilities they consider, the greater is the effort needed to focus their attention single-mindedly on one stroke. Of course, some positions do call for a lot of thought but how many breaks over 40 have you ever seen at snooker when there has been a one or two minute interval between each shot? One of the biggest handicaps in being a slow player is the consequent lack of rhythm and fluency. The longer you take between shots, the more chance there is of your mind wondering to some more or less irrelevant issue. In trying to take that extra bit of care, you may allow a thought into your head like 'I've only got to take the next few balls and I've won,' or if in play with a 70-odd break, 'I've got a chance of a century here.' As soon as you start dissipating your concentration like this, something is bound to go wrong. The ideal aim is to pack a very intense concentration into a fairly short time.

Here, I may draw an analogy with a

moving ball game – tennis. Sometimes, at Wimbledon say, you see a player hit a fantastic winner off a ball that looks as if it has beaten him all the way. Hitting that winner is what you might call a reflex action. If the player had to think about getting his right foot in such a position, his left foot in another, turning half sideways to the ball, altering his grip on the racket, and a hundred other things, he would never hit such a good shot in a month of Sundays. No, what happens, is that his eye observes a certain situation (the ball coming towards him) and his body, conditioned to playing the game a great deal, responds to it more or less automatically (by hitting it with his racket).

Many good players have the same sort of approach to billiards and snooker. Their eye observes a certain position and through experience and practice they almost automatically select and play the right shot. They do not think: 'I will hit this ball at such and such an angle, with so much side and so much screw, taking great care that my cue comes through straight, that the line from my elbow to my wrist is perfectly straight, that my bridge is perfectly still . . .' No, they assess shots subconsciously and more or less wordlessly. Some shots, of course, require a more conscious reasoning approach.

The more you can think subconsciously in a special kind of 'snooker language' if you like, the better your concentration is likely to be.

In commending 'quick and decisive' play, Mr Longhurst rightly says that it is equally important to formulate 'a kind of drill, which never varies, however intense the pressure.' At snooker or billiards you will never attain any kind of rhythm if you spend ten seconds over one shot, two minutes over the next, half a minute over the next and so on. If you can manage to play at a steady regular pace your game will tend to blend harmoniously together instead of looking and feeling like a series of islated unrelated shots.

Perhaps I should sum up on the most important points. These are:

(1) Make sure that you keep perfectly steady when you are hitting the cue-ball. In particular, keep your bridge hand steady.

(2) Do your thinking beforehand and not during a shot. If you alter your mind about using side, for instance, take up a fresh stance and start again.

(3) Be quick, decisive and mentally alert in your approach to the game.

(4) Treat every shot on its merits. If you have to pot an easy black off its spot to win the Amateur Championship, don't feather at it ten seconds longer than you would if you had the same shot in a league match.

(5) Make a real effort to attain rhythm and fluency. If you manage this, you will make breaks with far less effort.

(6) Most important of all, try to cultivate an intense concentration. Many players are habitual bad starters because they need time really to focus their concentration on the game. Some other players tend to start well and then deteriorate either because they begin to congratulate themselves on a good shot or worry over a bad one. They dissipate their concentration and their game goes to pieces.

Finally, a word about a mental barrier which still upsets a lot of good players – the 100 break barrier. This is less a problem than it used to be since it is no longer all that unusual for an amateur to make a century but there are still very few players who do not feel some nervousness when they approach their first century.

One amateur I know made 14 breaks over 90 before he made his first century, but I was very lucky in that I made my first century when my previous highest break was only 69. This meant that I had never really come near enough to a century for me to feel any immediate compulsive ambition to make one. I therefore made my first century without giving the actual figure 100 much serious thought. If, on the other hand, I had already had a near miss or two, I would probably, even with the balls identically situated, have been a bundle of nerves and have failed to reach three figures.

Most players when they are in sight of their first century have a tendency to try too hard. Instead of playing each shot on its merits, the player gives way to such thoughts as 'Can I do it?' . . . 'Only four more balls to go' . . . and so on. He gets a little bit too excited thinking how nice it would be if he could manage a century (which is the best way in the world to divert his concentration from the actual playing of the shot) and, consequently, he breaks down. On the other hand, if you already have a century or two behind you it is much easier to keep your game steady, and avoid unnecessary – and in a sense irrelevant – tension.

I think the best advice I can give to anyone just on the verge of breaking through a mental barrier (and making frequent 80s and 90s without making any centuries represents very much more a mental barrier than any deficiency in technique) is to try to relax as much as possible. Make every effort to convince yourself that it doesn't matter at all that much if you don't make a century. You never will succeed in convincing yourself but if you make the effort and trust yourself just to play the shots, as they come, to the best of your ability, the chances

are that you will find that vital element of relaxation which makes all the difference between solid achievement and nervy near misses.

Before I leave this subject though I would like to touch on two points. Firstly, it would not be true to say that the only reason every 90 is not a 100 is a mental one. I myself still find that I make roughly five 90s for every 100, mainly because the most difficult reds tend to be left until after easier ones have been potted but also to some extent because many breaks end because no balls remain on the table. Secondly, do not forget that, except for exhibition play, breaks are only means to an end. I was playing Fred Davis once when somebody started chatting to him at the end of the session. In due course, he asked Fred what his highest break was. '143' said Fred. 'Oh' said the spectator. 'Joe's is 147, isn't it?' 'It still only won him one frame,' said Fred.

Though Fred meant this as a joke, of course, his remark implied the important principle that the object of the game is to win and that big breaks are but a means to this end.

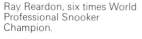
Ray Reardon, six times World Professional Snooker Champion.

Chapter Fourteen
A Century Break Analysed

I have made over 1,000 century breaks at snooker and one which sticks out in my mind as one of, if not the, hardest I have ever made was against golf professional David Craike at the Salisbury Club, Henley-on-Thames. This break of 101 contained more obstacles and gave me more satisfaction than many a break of 120 or even 130 – and that is saying something!.

Figure 109 shows the position of the balls when my break had reached 43. All the colours except the pink were on their spots and most of the remaining reds were trickily placed. I have numbered the reds in the order in which I potted them. The previous shot I had potted the blue and tried to leave myself the pot which Figure 109, Shot 1 shows. As you can see, there was not much margin of error in playing to obtain position on this red but I did know that, at the worst, I had a 'saver' in an easy red lying over the middle pocket. As it happened, however, I obtained the position I played for and, as shown in the diagram, I duly potted the red.

This brought me on to the blue again (Figure 109, Shot 2) but, at such an angle that I could not get position on the easy red by the middle pocket but had, instead, to play for a double. I managed to pull off the double (Figure 109, Shot 3) and, using screw and left-hand side, knocked the other red which was lying under that cushion towards the top pocket.

I could, of course, have played the double plain ball, and have attempted to gain position on the blue or black, but, as the other red had to be disturbed from its position anyway, this was an ideal opportunity to do so.

The advantage of using left-hand (running) side, as I did was that the cue-ball did not stop almost as soon as it had contacted the second red – as it would have done, had the fullish contact been made with no side or check side – but was instead able to gather momentum with the spin. This enabled the cue-ball to finish in a fairly good position on the black.

Figure 110 shows first (Shot 1) how I potted the black, to bring my break to 57, but also how I did not play quite hard enough to gain an ideal position on the next red. True, I was still able to pot it but the angle was too fine for me comfortably to be able to stay on the black.

I therefore played this thin pot with screw and right-hand side (Shot 2) but the cue-ball travelled a little further than I had intended and came to rest the 'wrong' side of the blue, which I potted but was thereby forced into playing red no. 14 thinly with left-hand side (to avoid the green) and coming round the cushions, as shown, to get on one of the baulk colours (Shot 3).

This gave me the chance to pot the brown and knock the last red into the open (Shot 4). As it was, the shot worked out as well as I could have hoped and I was able (Figure 111) to bring off the not-easy pot into the top left-hand pocket and run through slightly for position on the blue.

Figure 112, Shot 1, shows me playing the blue which brought my break to 74. As you can see, the pot itself was not difficult but the difficulty of getting in and out of baulk between the brown and the green had to be surmounted. As the diagram shows quite well, the main secret of this type of shot is gauging the amount of side in such a way that the cue-ball comes out of baulk on very nearly the same line as it goes in. I know this sounds easier than it is and the only way to gain any mastery of the shot is, of course, to practise it. One of the less obvious but very important things the shot required is an exact knowledge of how much side you are using.

The position shown, when Shot 1

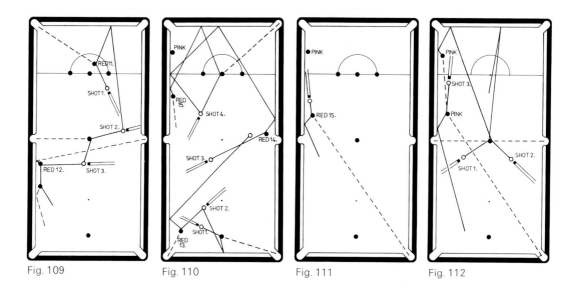

Fig. 109   Fig. 110   Fig. 111   Fig. 112

Steve Davis, World
Professional Snooker
Champion, 1981.

in Figure 112 had been played leaves me perfectly placed to take the yellow, green and brown and Shot 2 in the diagram shows me taking the blue and attempting to 'cannon' pink into the open. Finally, Shot 3 in Figure 112 shows me potting the pink to bring the break to 94 and leaving myself nicely on black to bring it to 101.

Looking back on the break, almost any one of the series of shots I have described could have gone wrong, the break containing, as it did, one double, three cannons, at least three difficult pots and innumerable positional difficulties. Nevertheless, it is one of the delights of the game that there are times when everything seems to 'come off'. They certainly make up for those occasions when something seems to go wrong with the most straightforward of positions.

Chapter Fifteen
How Billiards Helps Snooker

It is sad to see more and more players specializing in either billiards or snooker instead of trying to play both. Many players, of course, are so pressed for time that they feel they have insufficient time to play one game properly, let alone two, but there are also a great number of players with ample time for practice who specialize more or less exclusively in one game without realizing how helpful the other game could be to it.

Billiards is more helpful to snooker than snooker is to billiards but I will deal with the latter first. Snooker helps billiards mainly in two ways. Because there is generally more margin of error in billiards than snooker, one's cue-action can tend to become a little lazy or floppy. If this has in fact happened, snooker will show it up and you can begin to do something about it.

The other main way snooker can help billiards is to increase confidence in potting. Those who play billiards more or less exclusively (especially those players who score the bulk of their points by in-offs) gradually get out of touch at potting. Lack of practice at potting breeds lack of confidence and these players gradually find themselves playing all sorts of shots in preference to risking a pot. But everybody is forced into playing pots at snooker and, funnily enough, even people who pot very badly at billiards pot a little better at snooker.

Of course, even some of the players who are pretty near the top at amateur billiards, have such suspect cue-actions that it would be impossible for them to play top-class snooker. Naturally, it would be madness for these to switch their main attention from billiards but a few games of snooker from time to time would, I am convinced, do them no harm.

But the good which snooker does for billiards players is comparatively insignificant compared with the good billiards does for snooker players. Joe Davis has always said that he could never have attained the precision in his cue-ball control (only ever matched, I think, by his brother Fred at his peak) without an apprenticeship in billiards which encompassed innumerable thousand breaks. Even someone like John Pulman, who has never played a competitive professional billiards match, is an extremely useful billiards player, with a very solid and consistent red-ball game to back up his potting at the top of the table. John, in fact, begins every one of his practice sessions with some red ball play which he finds ideal for getting the cue-arm flowing smoothly and accurately.

However, a sound in-off game is useful to you not only for promoting a smooth cue action but for teaching you the 'angle of throw' which the cue-ball takes once it has contacted an object-ball. A good knowledge of the 'angle of throw' is essential for three main reasons.

First, it puts you on your guard against possible in-offs; second, it enables you to judge much better whether the cue-ball will, after it has contacted the object-ball, kiss another ball; and third, it enables you to make use of the natural angles in gaining position.

As a simple illustration of my first point I have drawn Figure 113. A plain-ball pot into the middle pocket involves an inevitable in-off in the corner pocket. This can easily be avoided if the danger is recognized by a little screw and possibly left-hand side but the player does need that little bit of billiards knowledge to recognize the danger. This, of course, is a very elementary example but the principle holds true in more advanced situations.

For instance, in Figure 114, a

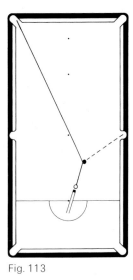

Fig. 113

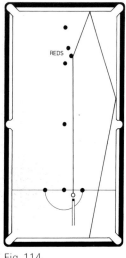

Fig. 114

'pure' snooker player is less likely than someone who plays billiards to know that it is quite possible to avoid an obvious looking in-off by contacting the red very thinly and returning to baulk. In other words, the billiards player, who has a thorough knowledge of the contacts needed to get in-offs is also, when he comes to play snooker, in a better position to avoid them.

This knowledge is also useful, of course, when the cue-ball has not only to avoid a pocket but other balls in order to finish in the desired position. In these cases, experience not only of in-offs but of cannons is helpful. In Figure 115, I have drawn a snooker position in which the striker is attempting a safety shot from the red marked 'A' off the cushion near red 'B' and back to somewhere near the baulk cushion, possibly to leave his opponent snookered behind the green.

What very commonly happens, however, when a player is attempting this is that an unintentional cannon is made with red 'B' but a billiards player, who is used to playing innumerable cannons off one, two or three cushions, is likely to have that extra knowledge which enables him to avoid the cannon when he wishes to. In short, there is nothing as good as billiards for improving your snookering and safety play and this, of course, is the reason why 'pure' billiards players can, when they do play snooker, make life sticky for a player whose potting and break-building may be far superior. However, as I have indicated, billiards can be useful in break-building too, as it is the best way I know for teaching you about the exact angle the cue-ball will take after it has contacted an object-ball, a vital thing to be aware of if aiming at good cue-ball control.

At snooker some people play for years, often with some success in local circles, without ever, or at least, rarely, giving the impression that they know where the cue-ball is going after it has contacted the ball they are trying to pot. In other words, they keep potting and hope for the best.

But, in billiards, it is impossible to make use of two of the three scoring media, namely the in-off and the cannon, **without** knowing the path the cue-ball is going to take after it has contacted the first object-ball. Therefore, other things being equal, the cue-ball control of the billiards **and snooker** player will be better than the man who plays snooker alone.

The man with billiards experience behind him starts with a great advantage in playing the return-to-baulk safety stroke. In Figure 116, there are two things to remember. First, the cue-ball must avoid the blue on its journey towards baulk and, second, it would be advantageous not only to finish as near the baulk cushion as possible, but to lay a snooker behind a conveniently situated colour, in this case, the yellow. To achieve the first part of this objective (avoiding the blue) it is a big help to know how you would play the shot if you were aiming to hit the blue, as if it were the second object-ball of an indirect cannon. If you know how you would play the shot to **hit** the blue then it is a simple matter to make the necessary adjustment in aiming so that you play to **miss** the blue. This is achieved here by playing with strong left-hand side.

Similarly, in order to get the cue-ball behind the yellow – thus snookering your opponent – some experience in playing all-round cannons is invaluable. As you can see from the diagram, a billiards all-round cannon closely resembles a snooker return-to-baulk safety shot or snooker.

In Figure 117, Shot 1, the striker is about to pot a red but the angle is a tricky one as regards obtaining position on a colour. The shot to play here is to pot the red and screw back on to the edge of another red, as shown in the diagram. It is vital that the second red should be contacted on the side nearest baulk, as contact on the edge nearest the left-hand side cushion would leave the cue-ball very near the pink, forming a line nearly parallel to the top cushion. Therefore, to make sure this does not happen, concentrate on striking the cue-ball well below centre. However, do not strike too low as the cue-ball will then recoil from the first red at too straight an angle so that it may well fail to contact